Camping Planner, Journal & Logbook

For Your Best Camping, Glamping & Bushcraft 101 Outdoor Adventure

DEDICATION

This planner, journal, and logbook is for the first-time camper and the experienced outdoor adventurer. It is designed to help anyone spending time under the stars have a better camping experience. This material will help with planning, preparing, reviewing, and making every trip better than the last.

WHAT'S INCLUDED?

The first section is How To Use the materials, then there are six pages that are repeated to be used for up to 25 trips. The last few pages include the phases of camping from arriving to coming home, a four-step survival method, and finally, additional resources.

HOW TO USE

1) CAMPING TRIP PLANNING WORKSHEET
2) GEAR & EQUIPMENT PACKING CHECKLIST
3) PERSONAL ITEMS / FIRST AID KIT LIST
4) 4-DAY CAMPING MEAL PLANNER & SHOPPING LIST
5) POST-TRIP REVIEW
6) TRIP EXPERIENCES / PICTURES / NOTES

PRE-, DURING-, AND POST-TRIP STEPS
S.A.F.E. SURVIVAL™ METHODOLOGY
ADDITIONAL RESOURCES

HOW TO USE >

This is a working planner, journal, and logbook for your next and future outdoor camping adventures. The content, layout, and structure are based on comments and questions from thousands of social media subscribers and our YouTube videos with over one million views. It covers what you need for trip planning, gear and equipment, meals and snacks, and post-trip review and activities. This journal includes six pages repeated to use for several dozen trips. The last few pages are pre, during, and post trip actions, a survival process, and additional supporting materials.

1 Camping Trip Planning Worksheet

This is where to start for any adventure. Depending on the trip location, popularity of venue, and other variables, you will want to start planning and making reservations up to 6-12 months out to secure hard-to-get spots or sites. In other situations, if you have everything you need, you could fill this section out a few days or weeks before you go. This planning phase is critical, as it helps you answer the most important questions regarding any type of trip.

2 Gear & Equipment Packing Checklist

This section is designed to help you make sure you have all the right gear, equipment, and necessary items to make your trip spectacular. This section is based on avoiding the biggest mistakes in camping such as forgetting, leaving, or not bringing critical camping pieces. This page provides an extensive inventory of groupings of camping items, and the specific name of each piece. The page follows a proven process to first identify the item (or number of items) you want to bring, and strike through those you don't want to bring. Then, to make sure nothing is left behind, a second column to mark once the item is visually loaded in your vehicle.

3 Personal Items / First Aid Kit

In addition to the right gear and equipment you will also need to pack personal items. This page is a basic checklist of different things for the individual. This unisex checklist is a single line item listed under Hygiene Kit in the GEAR & EQUIPMENT CHECKLIST. To further help you complete your trip preparations there is a column for a basic First Aid Kit. Use this checklist for minimal emergency items and add more as necessary for each type of trip.

4 4-Day Meal Planning, Equipment, and Grocery List

Great meals make great camping! To be prepared and have everything for amazing meals, this section provides meal and snack planning for five times a day, and the equipment necessary to prepare or cook the meal. Based on the type of meal, there are sections to write in the ingredients for that meal that can be used as a mark-through checklist when shopping. Don't forget to mark the cooking equipment checklist for your cooking methods!

5 Post-Trip Review

This page is about documenting the trip and how to make future adventures better than the last. It focuses on capturing the actual experience and results. There are sections asking about the trip, followed by what worked, what didn't, and what could be changed or modified to make the next trip even better.

6 Trip Experiences, Photographs, and Notes

This page is designed to provide space for the physical capture of items gathered or activities from the trip. In addition, there is space to put photographs or mementos. Keepsakes to put in your journal include maps, postcards, trail guide maps, badges, and other things that can be attached or go inside a book. This page is a great way to remember to find tangible memories and experiences of a trip.

Pre-, During-, and Post-Trip Steps

There are three parts to a camping trip after planning and once you have arrived at your campsite. This page will help you with the first step – setting up camp. Then the second step – breaking camp. The third and final step and many times the most important, is post-trip storage.

S.A.F.E. Survival™ Methodology

This page has been added because camping and being outdoors have risks. Your best tool for managing those risks and to get out of a bad situation, or not letting an incident become a catastrophe, is HOW TO THINK. This is a methodology to think AND act to become safe or quickly get to safety. It can be followed on land or water.

Additional Resources

This section provides information, links, and access to more support tools and materials including our books, videos, and website that support this planner and journal. All materials are based off the book Camping, Glamping, & Bushcraft 101: The Ultimate 3 in 1 Handbook for Outdoor Camping Adventures

CAMPING TRIP PLANNING ▷

Ready for your next great outdoor adventure? Use this worksheet to plan your trip and have the greatest "under the stars" experience possible.

What type of trip?

☐ Camping
☐ Tent Glamping
☐ Bushcraft
☐ Backpacking
☐ Combination

Why are you going?

☐ Fun
☐ Activities
☐ Alone Time
☐ Relaxation
☐ Develop and Test New Skills
☐ Others
_____

When will you go on your trip? Dates _____ to _____

Season _____ Seasonal Concerns _____

Location

City _____ ST _____ Park Name _____

Reservations Required? ☐ Yes ☐ No   ☐ Phone ☐ Web

Reservation # _____

Who is going? Name(s)

_____   _____
_____   _____

New Camping Skills and Preparation (Pitching Tent, Shelter Building, Fire Starting, Cooking, Hunting, Scavenging, Trapping, etc.) **Preparation** (Read, videos, testing, training, certification, etc.)

• Skill _____ How will you prep/test? _____
• Skill _____ How will you prep/test? _____

Special Gear/Equipment (New Type of Tent, Gas Equipment, Generator, Backpacks, Hunting, etc.)

1 _____   2 _____   3 _____

Gear to be purchased, rented or repaired?

1. Type of Gear _____ Purchase, rented, repaired? _____
2. Type of Gear _____ Purchase, rented, repaired? _____

How are you prepared for rain, cold, heat, wind, bugs and varmints?

Rain _____   Cold/Heat _____
Bugs _____   Varmints/Bears _____

Major Activities – What are the different activities you will do?

	Activity	Location
Day 1	_____	_____
Day 2	_____	_____
Day 3	_____	_____
Day 4	_____	_____

Nearest Emergency Room or Help

Facility_____ Address _____ Phone _____ Hours _____

Who Knows You're Gone   Name _____ Phone _____ Email _____

GEAR AND EQUIPMENT CHECKLIST

This is a basic checklist for camping, glamping & bushcraft trips. There are categories and specific camping items. Put an "X" or number in the "#" column in red or blue ink. If you don't want to take an item, then strike through it (e.g. ~~Hammock~~). Once you've loaded an item, mark an X in the LD (Loaded) column. Blanks are for add-ons. **Bolded italicized** items are Bushcraft suggested.

Trip to _____ # Days _____

Trip Type ☐ Camp ☐ Glamp ☐ Bushcraft   Dates _____

Tent/Shelter	#	LD
Tent/Hammock		
Rainfly		
Tent carpet		
Groundsheet/Tarp		
Guy Lines/Stakes		
Mallet/Hammer		
Tent Repair Kit		
Broom/Dustpan		
Sleeping system		
Sleeping Bag		
Sleeping Pad		
Blanket		
Pillow		
Inside/Outside Rug		
Sleeping Cot		
Tent Fan/Heater		
Camp Equipment		
Shelter/Canopy		
Chair		
Table		
Gear		
Backpack/Bag		
Gear Bag		
Knife/Multi-Tool		
Shovel		
Rope		
Strap/Bungee Cords		
Compass		
First Aid Kit		
Saw/Hatchet/Ax		
Duct Tape		
Work Gloves		
Activities		
Hiking/Biking Gear		

Kitchen/Cooking	#	LD
Canopy/Tarp		
Camp Kitchen		
Portable Grill/Grate		
Gas/Electric Stove & Fuel		
Dutch Oven & DO Lifter		
Pots / Pans / Skillet		
Cooler		
Table		
Water Jug		
Trash Can & Bags		
Drink/Coffee Cups		
Charcoal & Starter		
Dish/Biodegradable Soap		
Clothe & Paper Towels		
Grill Utensils/Oven Mitt		
Pots/Dishes		
Mess Kit		
Aluminum Foil		
Big Cutting Knives		
Frying Pan/Spatula		
Coffee Pot/Press/Maker		
Bottle/Wine Opener		
Wipes		
Ice		
Campfire		
Local Firewood		
Matches/Lighter/Starter		
Fire Extinguisher		
Roasting Sticks		
Electrical		
Flashlight		
Headlamp/Floodlight		
Lantern Fuel/Electric		
Extension Cord		
Extra Batteries / Charger		
Activities		
Fishing Gear / Bait		

Personal	#	LD
GUYS		
Jacket/Coat		
Shirts		
Pants		
Shorts		
Underwear		
Hygiene Kit		
Hat / Visor		
Socks		
Shoes / Boots		
Rain Gear		
Swimwear		
Sleepwear		
GIRLS		
Jacket/Coat		
Shirts/Blouses		
Pants		
Shorts		
Underwear		
Hygiene Kit		
Hat/Visor		
Socks		
Shoes/Boots		
Rain Gear		
Swimwear		
Sleepwear		
Misc		
Sunscreen/Bug Spray		
Bath Cloth/Towels		
Sunglasses		
Bandana		
Binoculars		
Activities		
Board Games/Cards		

PERSONAL ITEMS / FIRST AID

This checklist is for packing personal items for hygiene, miscellaneous, and first aid. The personal item section is designed for 4 people. To add more adults or children, just make a line to the right of the item. Use blank spaces for additional items.

Personal Item	Camper #1 ✓	#	Camper #2 ✓	#	Camper #3 ✓	#	Camper #4 ✓	#
Soap								
Toothbrush								
Toothpaste								
Dental Floss								
Deodorant								
Shampoo/Conditioner								
Comb/Brush								
Tissues								
Razor								
Shaving Cream								
Hand Sanitizer								
Cotton Tips								
Lotion								
Mouthwash								
Dental Floss								
Chapstick/Lip Balm								
Toilet Paper								
Tweezers								
Sunscreen								
Insect Repellent								
Washcloth								
Towel								
Mirror								
Hair Dryer								
Contacts/Case								
Saline Solution								
Nail Clippers/File								
Ear Plugs								
Medications								

First Aid Kit Checklist

First Aid Item	✓	#
Band Aids		
Gauze Pads		
Antiseptic Wipes		
Hydrogen Peroxide		
Cotton Balls		
Sanitizer		
Tweezers		
Scissors		
Instant Cold/Hot Packs		
Latex Gloves		
Blanket		
Oral Thermometer		
Adhesive Tape		
Antibiotic Ointment		
Antihistamines		
Crepe Bandages		
Hydrocortisone		
Painkillers		
Safety Pins		
CPR Mouthpiece		
Alcohol Wipes		
Aspirin		
Calamine Lotion		
Splint		
Sterile Eye Dressings		
Medications		
Bandana/Wraps		
First Aid Manual		

4-DAY CAMPING MEAL PLANNER

Great meals make great camping! However, preparing and cooking meals outdoors requires accurate planning to have the right ingredients and equipment for culinary success. Here is a basic meal planning guide for each meal, ingredients, cooking equipment / methods, and grocery list items. Write "Travel" for meals not needed. Use 2 Sheets For 5+Days.

MEALS	TYPE OF MEAL/FOOD	COOKING METHOD	GROCERY ITEMS/LIST	✓
Example	Sandwiches / Chips / Fruits	SK/None	Bread, Cold Cuts, Chips, Fruits	✓
DAY 1 Breakfast				
Snack				
Lunch				
Snack				
Dinner				
Treat				
DAY 2 Breakfast				
Snack				
Lunch				
Snack				
Dinner				
Treat				
DAY 3 Breakfast				
Snack				
Lunch				
Snack				
Dinner				
Treat				
DAY 4 Breakfast				
Snack				
Lunch				
Snack				
Dinner				
Treat				

*Cooking Methods: **(S)** Stove   **(G)** Grill   **(F)** Firepit   **(D)** Dutch Oven   **(H)** Hanging Pot   **(Sk)** Skillet

Drinks   ☐ Milk   ☐ Soda   ☐ Tea   ☐ Coffee   ☐ Drink Mix

Spices	**Condiments**	**Fruit**	**Nuts/Mix**	**Fixings**
☐ Salt	☐ Ketchup	☐ Apples	☐ Nuts/Seeds	☐ Lettuce
☐ Pepper	☐ Mustard	☐ Bananas	☐ Trail Mix	☐ Tomatoes
☐ Sugar	☐ Relish	☐ Oranges	☐ Power Bars	☐ Pickes
☐ Hot Sauce	☐ Salsa	☐ Grapefruit	☐ Fruit Bars	☐ Onions
☐ _____	☐ _____	☐ _____	☐ _____	☐ _____

POST-TRIP REVIEW

To make every camping trip better, it's important to capture and review what you liked and what you would change. Use this sheet to review and plan your next adventure.

Campground Name _____ Dates _____ To _____

Address Street _____ City _____ State _____

Type of Site/Park ☐ National ☐ State ☐ Private Campsite # _____

Types of Campsite ☐ Managed/RV ☐ Primitive ☐ Boondocking ☐ Wilderness

Types of Trip ☐ Basic Camping ☐ Glamping (Tent/Rental/RV)
                  ☐ Bushcraft ☐ Primitive ☐ Combination

Sites/Excursions Along the Way

1 _____ 2 _____ 3 _____

Designated Tent / Pad Sites? ☐ Yes ☐ No Campsite # _____

Campground Amenities

☐ Drinking Water (close/far)   ☐ Picnic   ☐ Firewood For Sale
☐ Fire Pits/Ring   ☐ Table – RV (120V 50A/30A)   ☐ Pet Friendly
☐ Tent Pads   ☐ Hookups   ☐ Nice Town
☐ BBQ Grill   ☐ Campground Store

What You Liked / What Went Well?

1 _____

2 _____

Other _____ Restrooms: Yes / No – Close / Far – Clean / Unclean – Shower / Electricity

What You Didn't Like / What Would You Change?

1 _____

2 _____

Animal Sightings _____

Biggest Surprise OR Need That The Campground Had (Or Didn't Have)?_____

Types of Activities Did You Do? (In Tent, Campsite, Campground, Local Areas, etc.)

_____

Things (activities / side trips) To Do Next Time?

_____

People You Met?

Name _____ From City/State _____ Phone/Email _____
Name _____ From City/State _____ Phone/Email _____
Name _____ From City/State _____ Phone/Email _____

TRIP EXPERIENCES

Notes

_____

_____

_____

_____

_____

CAMPING TRIP PLANNING

Ready for your next great outdoor adventure? Use this worksheet to plan your trip and have the greatest "under the stars" experience possible.

What type of trip?

☐ Camping
☐ Tent Glamping
☐ Bushcraft
☐ Backpacking
☐ Combination

Why are you going?

☐ Fun
☐ Activities
☐ Alone Time
☐ Relaxation
☐ Develop and Test New Skills
☐ Others
_____

When will you go on your trip? Dates _____ to _____

Season _____ Seasonal Concerns _____

Location

City _____ ST _____ Park Name _____

Reservations Required? ☐ Yes ☐ No   ☐ Phone ☐ Web

Reservation # _____

Who is going? Name(s)

_____ _____
_____ _____

New Camping Skills and Preparation (Pitching Tent, Shelter Building, Fire Starting, Cooking, Hunting, Scavenging, Trapping, etc.) **Preparation** (Read, videos, testing, training, certification, etc.)

• Skill _____ How will you prep/test? _____
• Skill _____ How will you prep/test? _____

Special Gear/Equipment (New Type of Tent, Gas Equipment, Generator, Backpacks, Hunting, etc.)

1 _____ 2 _____ 3 _____

Gear to be purchased, rented or repaired?

1. Type of Gear _____ Purchase, rented, repaired? _____
2. Type of Gear _____ Purchase, rented, repaired? _____

How are you prepared for rain, cold, heat, wind, bugs and varmints?

Rain _____ Cold/Heat _____
Bugs _____ Varmints/Bears _____

Major Activities – What are the different activities you will do?

	Activity	Location
Day 1	_____	_____
Day 2	_____	_____
Day 3	_____	_____
Day 4	_____	_____

Nearest Emergency Room or Help

Facility_____ Address _____ Phone _____ Hours _____

Who Knows You're Gone Name _____ Phone _____ Email _____

GEAR AND EQUIPMENT CHECKLIST

This is a basic checklist for camping, glamping & bushcraft trips. There are categories and specific camping items. Put an "X" or number in the "#" column in red or blue ink. If you don't want to take an item, then strike through it (e.g. ~~Hammock~~). Once you've loaded an item, mark an X in the LD (Loaded) column. Blanks are for add-ons. **Bolded italicized** items are Bushcraft suggested.

Trip to _____ # Days _____

Trip Type ☐ Camp   ☐ Glamp   ☐ Bushcraft   Dates _____

Tent/Shelter	#	LD
Tent/Hammock		
Rainfly		
Tent carpet		
Groundsheet/Tarp		
Guy Lines/Stakes		
Mallet/Hammer		
Tent Repair Kit		
Broom/Dustpan		
Sleeping system		
Sleeping Bag		
Sleeping Pad		
Blanket		
Pillow		
Inside/Outside Rug		
Sleeping Cot		
Tent Fan/Heater		
Camp Equipment		
Shelter/Canopy		
Chair		
Table		
Gear		
Backpack/Bag		
Gear Bag		
Knife/Multi-Tool		
Shovel		
Rope		
Strap/Bungee Cords		
Compass		
First Aid Kit		
Saw/Hatchet/Ax		
Duct Tape		
Work Gloves		
Activities		
Hiking/Biking Gear		

Kitchen/Cooking	#	LD
Canopy/Tarp		
Camp Kitchen		
Portable Grill/Grate		
Gas/Electric Stove & Fuel		
Dutch Oven & DO Lifter		
Pots / Pans / Skillet		
Cooler		
Table		
Water Jug		
Trash Can & Bags		
Drink/Coffee Cups		
Charcoal & Starter		
Dish/Biodegradable Soap		
Clothe & Paper Towels		
Grill Utensils/Oven Mitt		
Pots/Dishes		
Mess Kit		
Aluminum Foil		
Big Cutting Knives		
Frying Pan/Spatula		
Coffee Pot/Press/Maker		
Bottle/Wine Opener		
Wipes		
Ice		
Campfire		
Local Firewood		
Matches/Lighter/Starter		
Fire Extinguisher		
Roasting Sticks		
Electrical		
Flashlight		
Headlamp/Floodlight		
Lantern Fuel/Electric		
Extension Cord		
Extra Batteries / Charger		
Activities		
Fishing Gear / Bait		

Personal	#	LD
GUYS		
Jacket/Coat		
Shirts		
Pants		
Shorts		
Underwear		
Hygiene Kit		
Hat / Visor		
Socks		
Shoes / Boots		
Rain Gear		
Swimwear		
Sleepwear		
GIRLS		
Jacket/Coat		
Shirts/Blouses		
Pants		
Shorts		
Underwear		
Hygiene Kit		
Hat/Visor		
Socks		
Shoes/Boots		
Rain Gear		
Swimwear		
Sleepwear		
Misc		
Sunscreen/Bug Spray		
Bath Cloth/Towels		
Sunglasses		
Bandana		
Binoculars		
Activities		
Board Games/Cards		

PERSONAL ITEMS / FIRST AID

This checklist is for packing personal items for hygiene, miscellaneous, and first aid. The personal item section is designed for 4 people. To add more adults or children, just make a line to the right of the item. Use blank spaces for additional items.

Personal Item	Camper #1 ✓ | #	Camper #2 ✓ | #	Camper #3 ✓ | #	Camper #4 ✓ | #
Soap				
Toothbrush				
Toothpaste				
Dental Floss				
Deodorant				
Shampoo/Conditioner				
Comb/Brush				
Tissues				
Razor				
Shaving Cream				
Hand Sanitizer				
Cotton Tips				
Lotion				
Mouthwash				
Dental Floss				
Chapstick/Lip Balm				
Toilet Paper				
Tweezers				
Sunscreen				
Insect Repellent				
Washcloth				
Towel				
Mirror				
Hair Dryer				
Contacts/Case				
Saline Solution				
Nail Clippers/File				
Ear Plugs				
Medications				

First Aid Kit Checklist

First Aid Item	✓ | #
Band Aids	
Gauze Pads	
Antiseptic Wipes	
Hydrogen Peroxide	
Cotton Balls	
Sanitizer	
Tweezers	
Scissors	
Instant Cold/Hot Packs	
Latex Gloves	
Blanket	
Oral Thermometer	
Adhesive Tape	
Antibiotic Ointment	
Antihistamines	
Crepe Bandages	
Hydrocortisone	
Painkillers	
Safety Pins	
CPR Mouthpiece	
Alcohol Wipes	
Aspirin	
Calamine Lotion	
Splint	
Sterile Eye Dressings	
Medications	
Bandana/Wraps	
First Aid Manual	

4-DAY CAMPING MEAL PLANNER

Great meals make great camping! However, preparing and cooking meals outdoors requires accurate planning to have the right ingredients and equipment for culinary success. Here is a basic meal planning guide for each meal, ingredients, cooking equipment / methods, and grocery list items. Write "Travel" for meals not needed. Use 2 Sheets For 5+Days.

MEALS	TYPE OF MEAL/FOOD	COOKING METHOD	GROCERY ITEMS/LIST	✓
Example	Sandwiches / Chips / Fruits	SK/None	Bread, Cold Cuts, Chips, Fruits	✓
DAY 1 Breakfast				
Snack				
Lunch				
Snack				
Dinner				
Treat				
DAY 2 Breakfast				
Snack				
Lunch				
Snack				
Dinner				
Treat				
DAY 3 Breakfast				
Snack				
Lunch				
Snack				
Dinner				
Treat				
DAY 4 Breakfast				
Snack				
Lunch				
Snack				
Dinner				
Treat				

*Cooking Methods: **(S)** Stove **(G)** Grill **(F)** Firepit **(D)** Dutch Oven **(H)** Hanging Pot **(Sk)** Skillet

Drinks ☐ Milk ☐ Soda ☐ Tea ☐ Coffee ☐ Drink Mix

Spices	**Condiments**	**Fruit**	**Nuts/Mix**	**Fixings**
☐ Salt	☐ Ketchup	☐ Apples	☐ Nuts/Seeds	☐ Lettuce
☐ Pepper	☐ Mustard	☐ Bananas	☐ Trail Mix	☐ Tomatoes
☐ Sugar	☐ Relish	☐ Oranges	☐ Power Bars	☐ Pickes
☐ Hot Sauce	☐ Salsa	☐ Grapefruit	☐ Fruit Bars	☐ Onions
☐ _____	☐ _____	☐ _____	☐ _____	☐ _____

POST-TRIP REVIEW

To make every camping trip better, it's important to capture and review what you liked and what you would change. Use this sheet to review and plan your next adventure.

Campground Name _____ Dates _____ To _____

Address Street _____ City _____ State _____

Type of Site/Park ☐ National ☐ State ☐ Private Campsite # _____

Types of Campsite ☐ Managed/RV ☐ Primitive ☐ Boondocking ☐ Wilderness

Types of Trip ☐ Basic Camping ☐ Glamping (Tent/Rental/RV)
☐ Bushcraft ☐ Primitive ☐ Combination

Sites/Excursions Along the Way

1 _____ 2 _____ 3 _____

Designated Tent / Pad Sites? ☐ Yes ☐ No Campsite # _____

Campground Amenities

☐ Drinking Water (close/far)   ☐ Picnic   ☐ Firewood For Sale
☐ Fire Pits/Ring   ☐ Table – RV (120V 50A/30A)   ☐ Pet Friendly
☐ Tent Pads   ☐ Hookups   ☐ Nice Town
☐ BBQ Grill   ☐ Campground Store

What You Liked / What Went Well?

1 _____

2 _____

Other _____ Restrooms: Yes / No – Close / Far – Clean / Unclean – Shower / Electricity

What You Didn't Like / What Would You Change?

1 _____

2 _____

Animal Sightings _____

Biggest Surprise OR Need That The Campground Had (Or Didn't Have)?_____

Types of Activities Did You Do? (In Tent, Campsite, Campground, Local Areas, etc.)

_____

Things (activities / side trips) To Do Next Time?

_____

People You Met?

Name _____ From City/State _____ Phone/Email _____

Name _____ From City/State _____ Phone/Email _____

Name _____ From City/State _____ Phone/Email _____

TRIP EXPERIENCES

Notes

CAMPING TRIP PLANNING

Ready for your next great outdoor adventure? Use this worksheet to plan your trip and have the greatest "under the stars" experience possible.

What type of trip?

☐ Camping
☐ Tent Glamping
☐ Bushcraft
☐ Backpacking
☐ Combination

Why are you going?

☐ Fun
☐ Activities
☐ Alone Time
☐ Relaxation
☐ Develop and Test New Skills
☐ Others
_____

When will you go on your trip? Dates _____ to _____

Season _____ Seasonal Concerns _____

Location

City _____ ST _____ Park Name _____

Reservations Required? ☐ Yes ☐ No   ☐ Phone ☐ Web

Reservation # _____

Who is going? Name(s)

_____   _____
_____   _____

New Camping Skills and Preparation (Pitching Tent, Shelter Building, Fire Starting, Cooking, Hunting, Scavenging, Trapping, etc.) **Preparation** (Read, videos, testing, training, certification, etc.)

• Skill _____ How will you prep/test? _____
• Skill _____ How will you prep/test? _____

Special Gear/Equipment (New Type of Tent, Gas Equipment, Generator, Backpacks, Hunting, etc.)

1 _____   2 _____   3 _____

Gear to be purchased, rented or repaired?

1. Type of Gear _____ Purchase, rented, repaired? _____
2. Type of Gear _____ Purchase, rented, repaired? _____

How are you prepared for rain, cold, heat, wind, bugs and varmints?

Rain _____   Cold/Heat _____
Bugs _____   Varmints/Bears _____

Major Activities – What are the different activities you will do?

	Activity	Location
Day 1	_____	_____
Day 2	_____	_____
Day 3	_____	_____
Day 4	_____	_____

Nearest Emergency Room or Help

Facility_____ Address _____ Phone _____ Hours _____

Who Knows You're Gone Name _____ Phone _____ Email _____

GEAR AND EQUIPMENT CHECKLIST

This is a basic checklist for camping, glamping & bushcraft trips. There are categories and specific camping items. Put an "X" or number in the "#" column in red or blue ink. If you don't want to take an item, then strike through it (e.g. ~~Hammock~~). Once you've loaded an item, mark an X in the LD (Loaded) column. Blanks are for add-ons. **Bolded italicized** items are Bushcraft suggested.

Trip to _____ # Days _____

Trip Type ☐ Camp ☐ Glamp ☐ Bushcraft Dates _____

Tent/Shelter	#	LD
Tent/Hammock		
Rainfly		
Tent carpet		
Groundsheet/Tarp		
Guy Lines/Stakes		
Mallet/Hammer		
Tent Repair Kit		
Broom/Dustpan		
Sleeping system		
Sleeping Bag		
Sleeping Pad		
Blanket		
Pillow		
Inside/Outside Rug		
Sleeping Cot		
Tent Fan/Heater		
Camp Equipment		
Shelter/Canopy		
Chair		
Table		
Gear		
Backpack/Bag		
Gear Bag		
Knife/Multi-Tool		
Shovel		
Rope		
Strap/Bungee Cords		
Compass		
First Aid Kit		
Saw/Hatchet/Ax		
Duct Tape		
Work Gloves		
Activities		
Hiking/Biking Gear		

Kitchen/Cooking	#	LD
Canopy/Tarp		
Camp Kitchen		
Portable Grill/Grate		
Gas/Electric Stove & Fuel		
Dutch Oven & DO Lifter		
Pots / Pans / Skillet		
Cooler		
Table		
Water Jug		
Trash Can & Bags		
Drink/Coffee Cups		
Charcoal & Starter		
Dish/Biodegradable Soap		
Clothe & Paper Towels		
Grill Utensils/Oven Mitt		
Pots/Dishes		
Mess Kit		
Aluminum Foil		
Big Cutting Knives		
Frying Pan/Spatula		
Coffee Pot/Press/Maker		
Bottle/Wine Opener		
Wipes		
Ice		
Campfire		
Local Firewood		
Matches/Lighter/Starter		
Fire Extinguisher		
Roasting Sticks		
Electrical		
Flashlight		
Headlamp/Floodlight		
Lantern Fuel/Electric		
Extension Cord		
Extra Batteries / Charger		
Activities		
Fishing Gear / Bait		

Personal	#	LD
GUYS		
Jacket/Coat		
Shirts		
Pants		
Shorts		
Underwear		
Hygiene Kit		
Hat / Visor		
Socks		
Shoes / Boots		
Rain Gear		
Swimwear		
Sleepwear		
GIRLS		
Jacket/Coat		
Shirts/Blouses		
Pants		
Shorts		
Underwear		
Hygiene Kit		
Hat/Visor		
Socks		
Shoes/Boots		
Rain Gear		
Swimwear		
Sleepwear		
Misc		
Sunscreen/Bug Spray		
Bath Cloth/Towels		
Sunglasses		
Bandana		
Binoculars		
Activities		
Board Games/Cards		

PERSONAL ITEMS / FIRST AID

This checklist is for packing personal items for hygiene, miscellaneous, and first aid. The personal item section is designed for 4 people. To add more adults or children, just make a line to the right of the item. Use blank spaces for additional items.

Personal Item	Camper #1 ✓	#	Camper #2 ✓	#	Camper #3 ✓	#	Camper #4 ✓	#
Soap								
Toothbrush								
Toothpaste								
Dental Floss								
Deodorant								
Shampoo/Conditioner								
Comb/Brush								
Tissues								
Razor								
Shaving Cream								
Hand Sanitizer								
Cotton Tips								
Lotion								
Mouthwash								
Dental Floss								
Chapstick/Lip Balm								
Toilet Paper								
Tweezers								
Sunscreen								
Insect Repellent								
Washcloth								
Towel								
Mirror								
Hair Dryer								
Contacts/Case								
Saline Solution								
Nail Clippers/File								
Ear Plugs								
Medications								

First Aid Kit Checklist

First Aid Item	✓	#
Band Aids		
Gauze Pads		
Antiseptic Wipes		
Hydrogen Peroxide		
Cotton Balls		
Sanitizer		
Tweezers		
Scissors		
Instant Cold/Hot Packs		
Latex Gloves		
Blanket		
Oral Thermometer		
Adhesive Tape		
Antibiotic Ointment		
Antihistamines		
Crepe Bandages		
Hydrocortisone		
Painkillers		
Safety Pins		
CPR Mouthpiece		
Alcohol Wipes		
Aspirin		
Calamine Lotion		
Splint		
Sterile Eye Dressings		
Medications		
Bandana/Wraps		
First Aid Manual		

4-DAY CAMPING MEAL PLANNER

Great meals make great camping! However, preparing and cooking meals outdoors requires accurate planning to have the right ingredients and equipment for culinary success. Here is a basic meal planning guide for each meal, ingredients, cooking equipment / methods, and grocery list items. Write "Travel" for meals not needed. Use 2 Sheets For 5+Days.

MEALS	TYPE OF MEAL/FOOD	COOKING METHOD	GROCERY ITEMS/LIST	✔
Example	Sandwiches / Chips / Fruits	SK/None	Bread, Cold Cuts, Chips, Fruits	✔
DAY 1 Breakfast				
Snack				
Lunch				
Snack				
Dinner				
Treat				
DAY 2 Breakfast				
Snack				
Lunch				
Snack				
Dinner				
Treat				
DAY 3 Breakfast				
Snack				
Lunch				
Snack				
Dinner				
Treat				
DAY 4 Breakfast				
Snack				
Lunch				
Snack				
Dinner				
Treat				

*Cooking Methods: **(S)** Stove   **(G)** Grill   **(F)** Firepit   **(D)** Dutch Oven   **(H)** Hanging Pot   **(Sk)** Skillet

Drinks   ☐ Milk   ☐ Soda   ☐ Tea   ☐ Coffee   ☐ Drink Mix

Spices	**Condiments**	**Fruit**	**Nuts/Mix**	**Fixings**
☐ Salt	☐ Ketchup	☐ Apples	☐ Nuts/Seeds	☐ Lettuce
☐ Pepper	☐ Mustard	☐ Bananas	☐ Trail Mix	☐ Tomatoes
☐ Sugar	☐ Relish	☐ Oranges	☐ Power Bars	☐ Pickes
☐ Hot Sauce	☐ Salsa	☐ Grapefruit	☐ Fruit Bars	☐ Onions
☐ _____	☐ _____	☐ _____	☐ _____	☐ _____

POST-TRIP REVIEW

To make every camping trip better, it's important to capture and review what you liked and what you would change. Use this sheet to review and plan your next adventure.

Campground Name _____ Dates _____ To _____

Address Street _____ City _____ State _____

Type of Site/Park ☐ National ☐ State ☐ Private Campsite # _____

Types of Campsite ☐ Managed/RV ☐ Primitive ☐ Boondocking ☐ Wilderness

Types of Trip ☐ Basic Camping ☐ Glamping (Tent/Rental/RV)
☐ Bushcraft ☐ Primitive ☐ Combination

Sites/Excursions Along the Way

1 _____ 2 _____ 3 _____

Designated Tent / Pad Sites? ☐ Yes ☐ No Campsite # _____

Campground Amenities

☐ Drinking Water (close/far) ☐ Picnic ☐ Firewood For Sale
☐ Fire Pits/Ring ☐ Table – RV (120V 50A/30A) ☐ Pet Friendly
☐ Tent Pads ☐ Hookups ☐ Nice Town
☐ BBQ Grill ☐ Campground Store

What You Liked / What Went Well?

1 _____

2 _____

Other _____ Restrooms: Yes / No – Close / Far – Clean / Unclean – Shower / Electricity

What You Didn't Like / What Would You Change?

1 _____

2 _____

Animal Sightings _____

Biggest Surprise OR Need That The Campground Had (Or Didn't Have)?_____

Types of Activities Did You Do? (In Tent, Campsite, Campground, Local Areas, etc.)

_____

Things (activities / side trips) To Do Next Time?

_____

People You Met?

Name _____ From City/State _____ Phone/Email _____
Name _____ From City/State _____ Phone/Email _____
Name _____ From City/State _____ Phone/Email _____

TRIP EXPERIENCES

Notes

_____

_____

_____

_____

_____

CAMPING TRIP PLANNING

Ready for your next great outdoor adventure? Use this worksheet to plan your trip and have the greatest "under the stars" experience possible.

What type of trip?

☐ Camping
☐ Tent Glamping
☐ Bushcraft
☐ Backpacking
☐ Combination

Why are you going?

☐ Fun
☐ Activities
☐ Alone Time
☐ Relaxation
☐ Develop and Test New Skills
☐ Others
_____

When will you go on your trip? Dates _____ to _____

Season _____ Seasonal Concerns _____

Location

City _____ ST _____ Park Name _____

Reservations Required? ☐ Yes ☐ No   ☐ Phone ☐ Web

Reservation # _____

Who is going? Name(s)

_____ _____
_____ _____

New Camping Skills and Preparation (Pitching Tent, Shelter Building, Fire Starting, Cooking, Hunting, Scavenging, Trapping, etc.) **Preparation** (Read, videos, testing, training, certification, etc.)

• Skill _____ How will you prep/test? _____
• Skill _____ How will you prep/test? _____

Special Gear/Equipment (New Type of Tent, Gas Equipment, Generator, Backpacks, Hunting, etc.)

1 _____   2 _____   3 _____

Gear to be purchased, rented or repaired?

1. Type of Gear _____ Purchase, rented, repaired? _____
2. Type of Gear _____ Purchase, rented, repaired? _____

How are you prepared for rain, cold, heat, wind, bugs and varmints?

Rain _____   Cold/Heat _____
Bugs _____   Varmints/Bears _____

Major Activities – What are the different activities you will do?

	Activity	Location
Day 1	_____	_____
Day 2	_____	_____
Day 3	_____	_____
Day 4	_____	_____

Nearest Emergency Room or Help

Facility _____ Address _____ Phone _____ Hours _____

Who Knows You're Gone Name _____ Phone _____ Email _____

GEAR AND EQUIPMENT CHECKLIST

This is a basic checklist for camping, glamping & bushcraft trips. There are categories and specific camping items. Put an "X" or number in the "#" column in red or blue ink. If you don't want to take an item, then strike through it (e.g. ~~Hammock~~). Once you've loaded an item, mark an X in the LD (Loaded) column. Blanks are for add-ons. **Bolded italicized** items are Bushcraft suggested.

Trip to _____ # Days _____

Trip Type ☐ Camp   ☐ Glamp   ☐ Bushcraft   Dates _____

Tent/Shelter	#	LD
Tent/Hammock		
Rainfly		
Tent carpet		
Groundsheet/Tarp		
Guy Lines/Stakes		
Mallet/Hammer		
Tent Repair Kit		
Broom/Dustpan		
Sleeping system		
Sleeping Bag		
Sleeping Pad		
Blanket		
Pillow		
Inside/Outside Rug		
Sleeping Cot		
Tent Fan/Heater		
Camp Equipment		
Shelter/Canopy		
Chair		
Table		
Gear		
Backpack/Bag		
Gear Bag		
Knife/Multi-Tool		
Shovel		
Rope		
Strap/Bungee Cords		
Compass		
First Aid Kit		
Saw/Hatchet/Ax		
Duct Tape		
Work Gloves		
Activities		
Hiking/Biking Gear		

Kitchen/Cooking	#	LD
Canopy/Tarp		
Camp Kitchen		
Portable Grill/Grate		
Gas/Electric Stove & Fuel		
Dutch Oven & DO Lifter		
Pots / Pans / Skillet		
Cooler		
Table		
Water Jug		
Trash Can & Bags		
Drink/Coffee Cups		
Charcoal & Starter		
Dish/Biodegradable Soap		
Clothe & Paper Towels		
Grill Utensils/Oven Mitt		
Pots/Dishes		
Mess Kit		
Aluminum Foil		
Big Cutting Knives		
Frying Pan/Spatula		
Coffee Pot/Press/Maker		
Bottle/Wine Opener		
Wipes		
Ice		
Campfire		
Local Firewood		
Matches/Lighter/Starter		
Fire Extinguisher		
Roasting Sticks		
Electrical		
Flashlight		
*Headlamp/*Floodlight		
Lantern Fuel/Electric		
Extension Cord		
Extra Batteries / Charger		
Activities		
Fishing Gear / Bait		

Personal	#	LD
GUYS		
Jacket/Coat		
Shirts		
Pants		
Shorts		
Underwear		
Hygiene Kit		
Hat / Visor		
Socks		
Shoes / Boots		
Rain Gear		
Swimwear		
Sleepwear		
GIRLS		
Jacket/Coat		
Shirts/Blouses		
Pants		
Shorts		
Underwear		
Hygiene Kit		
Hat/Visor		
Socks		
Shoes/Boots		
Rain Gear		
Swimwear		
Sleepwear		
Misc		
Sunscreen/Bug Spray		
Bath Cloth/Towels		
Sunglasses		
Bandana		
Binoculars		
Activities		
Board Games/Cards		

PERSONAL ITEMS / FIRST AID

This checklist is for packing personal items for hygiene, miscellaneous, and first aid. The personal item section is designed for 4 people. To add more adults or children, just make a line to the right of the item. Use blank spaces for additional items.

Personal Item	Camper #1 ✓ | #	Camper #2 ✓ | #	Camper #3 ✓ | #	Camper #4 ✓ | #
Soap				
Toothbrush				
Toothpaste				
Dental Floss				
Deodorant				
Shampoo/Conditioner				
Comb/Brush				
Tissues				
Razor				
Shaving Cream				
Hand Sanitizer				
Cotton Tips				
Lotion				
Mouthwash				
Dental Floss				
Chapstick/Lip Balm				
Toilet Paper				
Tweezers				
Sunscreen				
Insect Repellent				
Washcloth				
Towel				
Mirror				
Hair Dryer				
Contacts/Case				
Saline Solution				
Nail Clippers/File				
Ear Plugs				
Medications				

First Aid Kit Checklist

First Aid Item	✓ | #
Band Aids	
Gauze Pads	
Antiseptic Wipes	
Hydrogen Peroxide	
Cotton Balls	
Sanitizer	
Tweezers	
Scissors	
Instant Cold/Hot Packs	
Latex Gloves	
Blanket	
Oral Thermometer	
Adhesive Tape	
Antibiotic Ointment	
Antihistamines	
Crepe Bandages	
Hydrocortisone	
Painkillers	
Safety Pins	
CPR Mouthpiece	
Alcohol Wipes	
Aspirin	
Calamine Lotion	
Splint	
Sterile Eye Dressings	
Medications	
Bandana/Wraps	
First Aid Manual	

4-DAY CAMPING MEAL PLANNER

Great meals make great camping! However, preparing and cooking meals outdoors requires accurate planning to have the right ingredients and equipment for culinary success. Here is a basic meal planning guide for each meal, ingredients, cooking equipment / methods, and grocery list items. Write "Travel" for meals not needed. Use 2 Sheets For 5+Days.

MEALS	TYPE OF MEAL/FOOD	COOKING METHOD	GROCERY ITEMS/LIST	✔
Example	Sandwiches / Chips / Fruits	SK/None	Bread, Cold Cuts, Chips, Fruits	✔
DAY 1 Breakfast				
Snack				
Lunch				
Snack				
Dinner				
Treat				
DAY 2 Breakfast				
Snack				
Lunch				
Snack				
Dinner				
Treat				
DAY 3 Breakfast				
Snack				
Lunch				
Snack				
Dinner				
Treat				
DAY 4 Breakfast				
Snack				
Lunch				
Snack				
Dinner				
Treat				

*Cooking Methods: (S) Stove   (G) Grill   (F) Firepit   (D) Dutch Oven   (H) Hanging Pot   (Sk) Skillet

Drinks   ☐ Milk   ☐ Soda   ☐ Tea   ☐ Coffee   ☐ Drink Mix

Spices	**Condiments**	**Fruit**	**Nuts/Mix**	**Fixings**
☐ Salt	☐ Ketchup	☐ Apples	☐ Nuts/Seeds	☐ Lettuce
☐ Pepper	☐ Mustard	☐ Bananas	☐ Trail Mix	☐ Tomatoes
☐ Sugar	☐ Relish	☐ Oranges	☐ Power Bars	☐ Pickes
☐ Hot Sauce	☐ Salsa	☐ Grapefruit	☐ Fruit Bars	☐ Onions
☐ _____	☐ _____	☐ _____	☐ _____	☐ _____

POST-TRIP REVIEW

To make every camping trip better, it's important to capture and review what you liked and what you would change. Use this sheet to review and plan your next adventure.

Campground Name _____ Dates _____ To _____

Address Street _____ City _____ State _____

Type of Site/Park ☐ National ☐ State ☐ Private Campsite # _____

Types of Campsite ☐ Managed/RV ☐ Primitive ☐ Boondocking ☐ Wilderness

Types of Trip ☐ Basic Camping ☐ Glamping (Tent/Rental/RV)
☐ Bushcraft ☐ Primitive ☐ Combination

Sites/Excursions Along the Way

1 _____ 2 _____ 3 _____

Designated Tent / Pad Sites? ☐ Yes ☐ No Campsite # _____

Campground Amenities

☐ Drinking Water (close/far) ☐ Picnic ☐ Firewood For Sale
☐ Fire Pits/Ring ☐ Table – RV (120V 50A/30A) ☐ Pet Friendly
☐ Tent Pads ☐ Hookups ☐ Nice Town
☐ BBQ Grill ☐ Campground Store

What You Liked / What Went Well?

1 _____
2 _____

Other _____ Restrooms: Yes / No – Close / Far – Clean / Unclean – Shower / Electricity

What You Didn't Like / What Would You Change?

1 _____
2 _____

Animal Sightings _____

Biggest Surprise OR Need That The Campground Had (Or Didn't Have)? _____

Types of Activities Did You Do? (In Tent, Campsite, Campground, Local Areas, etc.)

_____

Things (activities / side trips) To Do Next Time?

_____

People You Met?

Name _____ From City/State _____ Phone/Email _____
Name _____ From City/State _____ Phone/Email _____
Name _____ From City/State _____ Phone/Email _____

Notes

_____

_____

_____

_____

_____

CAMPING TRIP PLANNING

Ready for your next great outdoor adventure? Use this worksheet to plan your trip and have the greatest "under the stars" experience possible.

What type of trip?

☐ Camping
☐ Tent Glamping
☐ Bushcraft
☐ Backpacking
☐ Combination

Why are you going?

☐ Fun
☐ Activities
☐ Alone Time
☐ Relaxation
☐ Develop and Test New Skills
☐ Others
_____

When will you go on your trip? Dates _____ to _____

Season _____ Seasonal Concerns _____

Location

City _____ ST _____ Park Name _____

Reservations Required? ☐ Yes ☐ No ☐ Phone ☐ Web

Reservation # _____

Who is going? Name(s)

_____   _____

_____   _____

New Camping Skills and Preparation (Pitching Tent, Shelter Building, Fire Starting, Cooking, Hunting, Scavenging, Trapping, etc.) **Preparation** (Read, videos, testing, training, certification, etc.)

- Skill _____ How will you prep/test? _____
- Skill _____ How will you prep/test? _____

Special Gear/Equipment (New Type of Tent, Gas Equipment, Generator, Backpacks, Hunting, etc.)

1 _____   2 _____   3 _____

Gear to be purchased, rented or repaired?

1. Type of Gear _____ Purchase, rented, repaired? _____
2. Type of Gear _____ Purchase, rented, repaired? _____

How are you prepared for rain, cold, heat, wind, bugs and varmints?

Rain _____   Cold/Heat _____

Bugs _____   Varmints/Bears _____

Major Activities – What are the different activities you will do?

	Activity	Location
Day 1	_____	_____
Day 2	_____	_____
Day 3	_____	_____
Day 4	_____	_____

Nearest Emergency Room or Help

Facility_____ Address _____ Phone _____ Hours _____

Who Knows You're Gone Name _____ Phone _____ Email _____

GEAR AND EQUIPMENT CHECKLIST

This is a basic checklist for camping, glamping & bushcraft trips. There are categories and specific camping items. Put an "X" or number in the "#" column in red or blue ink. If you don't want to take an item, then strike through it (e.g. ~~Hammock~~). Once you've loaded an item, mark an X in the LD (Loaded) column. Blanks are for add-ons. **Bolded italicized** items are Bushcraft suggested.

Trip to _____ # Days _____

Trip Type ☐ Camp ☐ Glamp ☐ Bushcraft Dates _____

Tent/Shelter	#	LD
Tent/Hammock		
Rainfly		
Tent carpet		
Groundsheet/Tarp		
Guy Lines/Stakes		
Mallet/Hammer		
Tent Repair Kit		
Broom/Dustpan		
Sleeping system		
Sleeping Bag		
Sleeping Pad		
Blanket		
Pillow		
Inside/Outside Rug		
Sleeping Cot		
Tent Fan/Heater		
Camp Equipment		
Shelter/Canopy		
Chair		
Table		
Gear		
Backpack/Bag		
Gear Bag		
Knife/Multi-Tool		
Shovel		
Rope		
Strap/Bungee Cords		
Compass		
First Aid Kit		
Saw/Hatchet/Ax		
Duct Tape		
Work Gloves		
Activities		
Hiking/Biking Gear		

Kitchen/Cooking	#	LD
Canopy/Tarp		
Camp Kitchen		
Portable Grill/Grate		
Gas/Electric Stove & Fuel		
Dutch Oven & DO Lifter		
Pots / Pans / Skillet		
Cooler		
Table		
Water Jug		
Trash Can & Bags		
Drink/Coffee Cups		
Charcoal & Starter		
Dish/Biodegradable Soap		
Clothe & Paper Towels		
Grill Utensils/Oven Mitt		
Pots/Dishes		
Mess Kit		
Aluminum Foil		
Big Cutting Knives		
Frying Pan/Spatula		
Coffee Pot/Press/Maker		
Bottle/Wine Opener		
Wipes		
Ice		
Campfire		
Local Firewood		
Matches/Lighter/Starter		
Fire Extinguisher		
Roasting Sticks		
Electrical		
Flashlight		
Headlamp/Floodlight		
Lantern Fuel/Electric		
Extension Cord		
Extra Batteries / Charger		
Activities		
Fishing Gear / Bait		

Personal	#	LD
GUYS		
Jacket/Coat		
Shirts		
Pants		
Shorts		
Underwear		
Hygiene Kit		
Hat / Visor		
Socks		
Shoes / Boots		
Rain Gear		
Swimwear		
Sleepwear		
GIRLS		
Jacket/Coat		
Shirts/Blouses		
Pants		
Shorts		
Underwear		
Hygiene Kit		
Hat/Visor		
Socks		
Shoes/Boots		
Rain Gear		
Swimwear		
Sleepwear		
Misc		
Sunscreen/Bug Spray		
Bath Cloth/Towels		
Sunglasses		
Bandana		
Binoculars		
Activities		
Board Games/Cards		

PERSONAL ITEMS / FIRST AID

This checklist is for packing personal items for hygiene, miscellaneous, and first aid. The personal item section is designed for 4 people. To add more adults or children, just make a line to the right of the item. Use blank spaces for additional items.

Personal Item	Camper #1 ✓ | #	Camper #2 ✓ | #	Camper #3 ✓ | #	Camper #4 ✓ | #
Soap				
Toothbrush				
Toothpaste				
Dental Floss				
Deodorant				
Shampoo/Conditioner				
Comb/Brush				
Tissues				
Razor				
Shaving Cream				
Hand Sanitizer				
Cotton Tips				
Lotion				
Mouthwash				
Dental Floss				
Chapstick/Lip Balm				
Toilet Paper				
Tweezers				
Sunscreen				
Insect Repellent				
Washcloth				
Towel				
Mirror				
Hair Dryer				
Contacts/Case				
Saline Solution				
Nail Clippers/File				
Ear Plugs				
Medications				

First Aid Kit Checklist

First Aid Item	✓ | #
Band Aids	
Gauze Pads	
Antiseptic Wipes	
Hydrogen Peroxide	
Cotton Balls	
Sanitizer	
Tweezers	
Scissors	
Instant Cold/Hot Packs	
Latex Gloves	
Blanket	
Oral Thermometer	
Adhesive Tape	
Antibiotic Ointment	
Antihistamines	
Crepe Bandages	
Hydrocortisone	
Painkillers	
Safety Pins	
CPR Mouthpiece	
Alcohol Wipes	
Aspirin	
Calamine Lotion	
Splint	
Sterile Eye Dressings	
Medications	
Bandana/Wraps	
First Aid Manual	

4-DAY CAMPING MEAL PLANNER

Great meals make great camping! However, preparing and cooking meals outdoors requires accurate planning to have the right ingredients and equipment for culinary success. Here is a basic meal planning guide for each meal, ingredients, cooking equipment / methods, and grocery list items. Write "Travel" for meals not needed. Use 2 Sheets For 5+Days.

	MEALS	TYPE OF MEAL/FOOD	COOKING METHOD	GROCERY ITEMS/LIST	✔
	Example	Sandwiches / Chips / Fruits	SK/None	Bread, Cold Cuts, Chips, Fruits	✔
DAY 1	Breakfast				
	Snack				
	Lunch				
	Snack				
	Dinner				
	Treat				
DAY 2	Breakfast				
	Snack				
	Lunch				
	Snack				
	Dinner				
	Treat				
DAY 3	Breakfast				
	Snack				
	Lunch				
	Snack				
	Dinner				
	Treat				
DAY 4	Breakfast				
	Snack				
	Lunch				
	Snack				
	Dinner				
	Treat				

*Cooking Methods: **(S)** Stove   **(G)** Grill   **(F)** Firepit   **(D)** Dutch Oven   **(H)** Hanging Pot   **(Sk)** Skillet

Drinks   ☐ Milk   ☐ Soda   ☐ Tea   ☐ Coffee   ☐ Drink Mix

Spices	**Condiments**	**Fruit**	**Nuts/Mix**	**Fixings**
☐ Salt	☐ Ketchup	☐ Apples	☐ Nuts/Seeds	☐ Lettuce
☐ Pepper	☐ Mustard	☐ Bananas	☐ Trail Mix	☐ Tomatoes
☐ Sugar	☐ Relish	☐ Oranges	☐ Power Bars	☐ Pickes
☐ Hot Sauce	☐ Salsa	☐ Grapefruit	☐ Fruit Bars	☐ Onions
☐ _____	☐ _____	☐ _____	☐ _____	☐ _____

POST-TRIP REVIEW

To make every camping trip better, it's important to capture and review what you liked and what you would change. Use this sheet to review and plan your next adventure.

Campground Name _____ Dates _____ To _____

Address Street _____ City _____ State _____

Type of Site/Park ☐ National ☐ State ☐ Private Campsite # _____

Types of Campsite ☐ Managed/RV ☐ Primitive ☐ Boondocking ☐ Wilderness

Types of Trip ☐ Basic Camping ☐ Glamping (Tent/Rental/RV)
☐ Bushcraft ☐ Primitive ☐ Combination

Sites/Excursions Along the Way

1 _____ 2 _____ 3 _____

Designated Tent / Pad Sites? ☐ Yes ☐ No Campsite # _____

Campground Amenities

☐ Drinking Water (close/far)   ☐ Picnic   ☐ Firewood For Sale
☐ Fire Pits/Ring   ☐ Table – RV (120V 50A/30A)   ☐ Pet Friendly
☐ Tent Pads   ☐ Hookups   ☐ Nice Town
☐ BBQ Grill   ☐ Campground Store

What You Liked / What Went Well?

1 _____
2 _____

Other _____ Restrooms: Yes / No – Close / Far – Clean / Unclean – Shower / Electricity

What You Didn't Like / What Would You Change?

1 _____
2 _____

Animal Sightings _____

Biggest Surprise OR Need That The Campground Had (Or Didn't Have)? _____

Types of Activities Did You Do? (In Tent, Campsite, Campground, Local Areas, etc.)

_____

Things (activities / side trips) To Do Next Time?

_____

People You Met?

Name _____ From City/State _____ Phone/Email _____
Name _____ From City/State _____ Phone/Email _____
Name _____ From City/State _____ Phone/Email _____

TRIP EXPERIENCES

Notes

CAMPING TRIP PLANNING

Ready for your next great outdoor adventure? Use this worksheet to plan your trip and have the greatest "under the stars" experience possible.

What type of trip?

- ☐ Camping
- ☐ Tent Glamping
- ☐ Bushcraft
- ☐ Backpacking
- ☐ Combination

Why are you going?

- ☐ Fun
- ☐ Activities
- ☐ Alone Time
- ☐ Relaxation
- ☐ Develop and Test New Skills
- ☐ Others
  _____

When will you go on your trip? Dates _____ to _____

Season _____ Seasonal Concerns _____

Location

City _____ ST _____ Park Name _____

Reservations Required? ☐ Yes ☐ No   ☐ Phone ☐ Web

Reservation # _____

Who is going? Name(s)

_____   _____

_____   _____

New Camping Skills and Preparation (Pitching Tent, Shelter Building, Fire Starting, Cooking, Hunting, Scavenging, Trapping, etc.) **Preparation** (Read, videos, testing, training, certification, etc.)

- • Skill _____ How will you prep/test? _____
- • Skill _____ How will you prep/test? _____

Special Gear/Equipment (New Type of Tent, Gas Equipment, Generator, Backpacks, Hunting, etc.)

1 _____   2 _____   3 _____

Gear to be purchased, rented or repaired?

1. Type of Gear _____ Purchase, rented, repaired? _____
2. Type of Gear _____ Purchase, rented, repaired? _____

How are you prepared for rain, cold, heat, wind, bugs and varmints?

Rain _____   Cold/Heat _____

Bugs _____   Varmints/Bears _____

Major Activities – What are the different activities you will do?

	Activity	Location
Day 1	_____	_____
Day 2	_____	_____
Day 3	_____	_____
Day 4	_____	_____

Nearest Emergency Room or Help

Facility_____ Address _____ Phone _____ Hours _____

Who Knows You're Gone Name _____ Phone _____ Email _____

GEAR AND EQUIPMENT CHECKLIST

This is a basic checklist for camping, glamping & bushcraft trips. There are categories and specific camping items. Put an "X" or number in the "#" column in red or blue ink. If you don't want to take an item, then strike through it (e.g. ~~Hammock~~). Once you've loaded an item, mark an X in the LD (Loaded) column. Blanks are for add-ons. **Bolded italicized** items are Bushcraft suggested.

Trip to _____   # Days _____

Trip Type   ☐ Camp   ☐ Glamp   ☐ Bushcraft   Dates _____

Tent/Shelter	#	LD
Tent/Hammock		
Rainfly		
Tent carpet		
Groundsheet/Tarp		
Guy Lines/Stakes		
Mallet/Hammer		
Tent Repair Kit		
Broom/Dustpan		
Sleeping system		
Sleeping Bag		
Sleeping Pad		
Blanket		
Pillow		
Inside/Outside Rug		
Sleeping Cot		
Tent Fan/Heater		
Camp Equipment		
Shelter/Canopy		
Chair		
Table		
Gear		
Backpack/Bag		
Gear Bag		
Knife/Multi-Tool		
Shovel		
Rope		
Strap/Bungee Cords		
Compass		
First Aid Kit		
Saw/Hatchet/Ax		
Duct Tape		
Work Gloves		
Activities		
Hiking/Biking Gear		

Kitchen/Cooking	#	LD
Canopy/Tarp		
Camp Kitchen		
Portable Grill/Grate		
Gas/Electric Stove & Fuel		
Dutch Oven & DO Lifter		
Pots / Pans / Skillet		
Cooler		
Table		
Water Jug		
Trash Can & Bags		
Drink/Coffee Cups		
Charcoal & Starter		
Dish/Biodegradable Soap		
Clothe & Paper Towels		
Grill Utensils/Oven Mitt		
Pots/Dishes		
Mess Kit		
Aluminum Foil		
Big Cutting Knives		
Frying Pan/Spatula		
Coffee Pot/Press/Maker		
Bottle/Wine Opener		
Wipes		
Ice		
Campfire		
Local Firewood		
Matches/Lighter/Starter		
Fire Extinguisher		
Roasting Sticks		
Electrical		
Flashlight		
Headlamp/Floodlight		
Lantern Fuel/Electric		
Extension Cord		
Extra Batteries / Charger		
Activities		
Fishing Gear / Bait		

Personal	#	LD
GUYS		
Jacket/Coat		
Shirts		
Pants		
Shorts		
Underwear		
Hygiene Kit		
Hat / Visor		
Socks		
Shoes / Boots		
Rain Gear		
Swimwear		
Sleepwear		
GIRLS		
Jacket/Coat		
Shirts/Blouses		
Pants		
Shorts		
Underwear		
Hygiene Kit		
Hat/Visor		
Socks		
Shoes/Boots		
Rain Gear		
Swimwear		
Sleepwear		
Misc		
Sunscreen/Bug Spray		
Bath Cloth/Towels		
Sunglasses		
Bandana		
Binoculars		
Activities		
Board Games/Cards		

PERSONAL ITEMS / FIRST AID

This checklist is for packing personal items for hygiene, miscellaneous, and first aid. The personal item section is designed for 4 people. To add more adults or children, just make a line to the right of the item. Use blank spaces for additional items.

Personal Item	Camper #1 ✓ | #	Camper #2 ✓ | #	Camper #3 ✓ | #	Camper #4 ✓ | #
Soap				
Toothbrush				
Toothpaste				
Dental Floss				
Deodorant				
Shampoo/Conditioner				
Comb/Brush				
Tissues				
Razor				
Shaving Cream				
Hand Sanitizer				
Cotton Tips				
Lotion				
Mouthwash				
Dental Floss				
Chapstick/Lip Balm				
Toilet Paper				
Tweezers				
Sunscreen				
Insect Repellent				
Washcloth				
Towel				
Mirror				
Hair Dryer				
Contacts/Case				
Saline Solution				
Nail Clippers/File				
Ear Plugs				
Medications				

First Aid Kit Checklist

First Aid Item	✓ | #
Band Aids	
Gauze Pads	
Antiseptic Wipes	
Hydrogen Peroxide	
Cotton Balls	
Sanitizer	
Tweezers	
Scissors	
Instant Cold/Hot Packs	
Latex Gloves	
Blanket	
Oral Thermometer	
Adhesive Tape	
Antibiotic Ointment	
Antihistamines	
Crepe Bandages	
Hydrocortisone	
Painkillers	
Safety Pins	
CPR Mouthpiece	
Alcohol Wipes	
Aspirin	
Calamine Lotion	
Splint	
Sterile Eye Dressings	
Medications	
Bandana/Wraps	
First Aid Manual	

4-DAY CAMPING MEAL PLANNER

Great meals make great camping! However, preparing and cooking meals outdoors requires accurate planning to have the right ingredients and equipment for culinary success. Here is a basic meal planning guide for each meal, ingredients, cooking equipment / methods, and grocery list items. Write "Travel" for meals not needed. Use 2 Sheets For 5+Days.

	MEALS	TYPE OF MEAL/FOOD	COOKING METHOD	GROCERY ITEMS/LIST	✓
	Example	Sandwiches / Chips / Fruits	SK/None	Bread, Cold Cuts, Chips, Fruits	✓
DAY 1	Breakfast				
	Snack				
	Lunch				
	Snack				
	Dinner				
	Treat				
DAY 2	Breakfast				
	Snack				
	Lunch				
	Snack				
	Dinner				
	Treat				
DAY 3	Breakfast				
	Snack				
	Lunch				
	Snack				
	Dinner				
	Treat				
DAY 4	Breakfast				
	Snack				
	Lunch				
	Snack				
	Dinner				
	Treat				

*Cooking Methods: **(S)** Stove   **(G)** Grill   **(F)** Firepit   **(D)** Dutch Oven   **(H)** Hanging Pot   **(Sk)** Skillet

Drinks   ☐ Milk   ☐ Soda   ☐ Tea   ☐ Coffee   ☐ Drink Mix

Spices	**Condiments**	**Fruit**	**Nuts/Mix**	**Fixings**
☐ Salt	☐ Ketchup	☐ Apples	☐ Nuts/Seeds	☐ Lettuce
☐ Pepper	☐ Mustard	☐ Bananas	☐ Trail Mix	☐ Tomatoes
☐ Sugar	☐ Relish	☐ Oranges	☐ Power Bars	☐ Pickes
☐ Hot Sauce	☐ Salsa	☐ Grapefruit	☐ Fruit Bars	☐ Onions
☐ _____	☐ _____	☐ _____	☐ _____	☐ _____

POST-TRIP REVIEW

To make every camping trip better, it's important to capture and review what you liked and what you would change. Use this sheet to review and plan your next adventure.

Campground Name _____ Dates _____ To _____

Address Street _____ City _____ State _____

Type of Site/Park ☐ National ☐ State ☐ Private Campsite # _____

Types of Campsite ☐ Managed/RV ☐ Primitive ☐ Boondocking ☐ Wilderness

Types of Trip ☐ Basic Camping ☐ Glamping (Tent/Rental/RV)
☐ Bushcraft ☐ Primitive ☐ Combination

Sites/Excursions Along the Way

1 _____ 2 _____ 3 _____

Designated Tent / Pad Sites? ☐ Yes ☐ No Campsite # _____

Campground Amenities

☐ Drinking Water (close/far)   ☐ Picnic   ☐ Firewood For Sale
☐ Fire Pits/Ring   ☐ Table – RV (120V 50A/30A)   ☐ Pet Friendly
☐ Tent Pads   ☐ Hookups   ☐ Nice Town
☐ BBQ Grill   ☐ Campground Store

What You Liked / What Went Well?

1 _____
2 _____

Other _____ Restrooms: Yes / No – Close / Far – Clean / Unclean – Shower / Electricity

What You Didn't Like / What Would You Change?

1 _____
2 _____

Animal Sightings _____

Biggest Surprise OR Need That The Campground Had (Or Didn't Have)? _____

Types of Activities Did You Do? (In Tent, Campsite, Campground, Local Areas, etc.)

_____

Things (activities / side trips) To Do Next Time?

_____

People You Met?

Name _____ From City/State _____ Phone/Email _____
Name _____ From City/State _____ Phone/Email _____
Name _____ From City/State _____ Phone/Email _____

Notes

_____

_____

_____

_____

_____

CAMPING TRIP PLANNING

Ready for your next great outdoor adventure? Use this worksheet to plan your trip and have the greatest "under the stars" experience possible.

What type of trip?

- ☐ Camping
- ☐ Tent Glamping
- ☐ Bushcraft
- ☐ Backpacking
- ☐ Combination

Why are you going?

- ☐ Fun
- ☐ Activities
- ☐ Alone Time
- ☐ Relaxation
- ☐ Develop and Test New Skills
- ☐ Others
- _____

When will you go on your trip? Dates _____ to _____

Season _____   Seasonal Concerns _____

Location

City _____   ST _____   Park Name _____

Reservations Required?   ☐ Yes ☐ No   ☐ Phone ☐ Web

Reservation # _____

Who is going? Name(s)

_____   _____
_____   _____

New Camping Skills and Preparation (Pitching Tent, Shelter Building, Fire Starting, Cooking, Hunting, Scavenging, Trapping, etc.) **Preparation** (Read, videos, testing, training, certification, etc.)

- Skill _____   How will you prep/test? _____
- Skill _____   How will you prep/test? _____

Special Gear/Equipment (New Type of Tent, Gas Equipment, Generator, Backpacks, Hunting, etc.)

1 _____   2 _____   3 _____

Gear to be purchased, rented or repaired?

1. Type of Gear _____   Purchase, rented, repaired? _____
2. Type of Gear _____   Purchase, rented, repaired? _____

How are you prepared for rain, cold, heat, wind, bugs and varmints?

Rain _____   Cold/Heat _____
Bugs _____   Varmints/Bears _____

Major Activities – What are the different activities you will do?

	Activity	Location
Day 1	_____	_____
Day 2	_____	_____
Day 3	_____	_____
Day 4	_____	_____

Nearest Emergency Room or Help

Facility_____   Address _____   Phone _____   Hours _____

Who Knows You're Gone   Name _____   Phone _____   Email _____

GEAR AND EQUIPMENT CHECKLIST

This is a basic checklist for camping, glamping & bushcraft trips. There are categories and specific camping items. Put an "X" or number in the "#" column in red or blue ink. If you don't want to take an item, then strike through it (e.g. ~~Hammock~~). Once you've loaded an item, mark an X in the LD (Loaded) column. Blanks are for add-ons. **Bolded italicized** items are Bushcraft suggested.

Trip to _____   # Days _____

Trip Type ☐ Camp   ☐ Glamp   ☐ Bushcraft   Dates _____

Tent/Shelter	#	LD	Kitchen/Cooking	#	LD	Personal	#	LD
Tent/Hammock			Canopy/Tarp			**GUYS**		
Rainfly			Camp Kitchen			*Jacket/Coat*		
Tent carpet			Portable Grill/Grate			*Shirts*		
Groundsheet/Tarp			Gas/Electric Stove & Fuel			*Pants*		
Guy Lines/Stakes			Dutch Oven & DO Lifter			*Shorts*		
Mallet/Hammer			*Pots / Pans / Skillet*			*Underwear*		
Tent Repair Kit			Cooler			*Hygiene Kit*		
Broom/Dustpan			Table			*Hat / Visor*		
			Water Jug			*Socks*		
			Trash Can & Bags			*Shoes / Boots*		
Sleeping system			Drink/Coffee Cups			*Rain Gear*		
Sleeping Bag			Charcoal & Starter			Swimwear		
Sleeping Pad			Dish/Biodegradable Soap			Sleepwear		
Blanket			Clothe & Paper Towels					
Pillow			Grill Utensils/Oven Mitt					
Inside/Outside Rug			Pots/Dishes			**GIRLS**		
Sleeping Cot			*Mess Kit*			*Jacket/Coat*		
Tent Fan/Heater			Aluminum Foil			*Shirts/Blouses*		
			Big Cutting Knives			*Pants*		
			Frying Pan/Spatula			*Shorts*		
Camp Equipment			Coffee Pot/Press/Maker			*Underwear*		
Shelter/Canopy			Bottle/Wine Opener			*Hygiene Kit*		
Chair			Wipes			*Hat/Visor*		
Table			Ice			*Socks*		
						Shoes/Boots		
Gear			**Campfire**			*Rain Gear*		
Backpack/Bag			Local Firewood			Swimwear		
Gear Bag			*Matches/Lighter/Starter*			Sleepwear		
Knife/Multi-Tool			Fire Extinguisher					
Shovel			Roasting Sticks					
Rope						**Misc**		
Strap/Bungee Cords			**Electrical**			Sunscreen/Bug Spray		
Compass			Flashlight			Bath Cloth/Towels		
First Aid Kit			*Headlamp*/Floodlight			Sunglasses		
Saw/Hatchet/Ax			Lantern Fuel/Electric			*Bandana*		
Duct Tape			*Extension Cord*			Binoculars		
Work Gloves			Extra Batteries / Charger					
Activities			**Activities**			**Activities**		
Hiking/Biking Gear			*Fishing Gear / Bait*			Board Games/Cards		

PERSONAL ITEMS / FIRST AID

This checklist is for packing personal items for hygiene, miscellaneous, and first aid. The personal item section is designed for 4 people. To add more adults or children, just make a line to the right of the item. Use blank spaces for additional items.

Personal Item	Camper #1 ✓	#	Camper #2 ✓	#	Camper #3 ✓	#	Camper #4 ✓	#
Soap								
Toothbrush								
Toothpaste								
Dental Floss								
Deodorant								
Shampoo/Conditioner								
Comb/Brush								
Tissues								
Razor								
Shaving Cream								
Hand Sanitizer								
Cotton Tips								
Lotion								
Mouthwash								
Dental Floss								
Chapstick/Lip Balm								
Toilet Paper								
Tweezers								
Sunscreen								
Insect Repellent								
Washcloth								
Towel								
Mirror								
Hair Dryer								
Contacts/Case								
Saline Solution								
Nail Clippers/File								
Ear Plugs								
Medications								

First Aid Kit Checklist

First Aid Item	✓	#
Band Aids		
Gauze Pads		
Antiseptic Wipes		
Hydrogen Peroxide		
Cotton Balls		
Sanitizer		
Tweezers		
Scissors		
Instant Cold/Hot Packs		
Latex Gloves		
Blanket		
Oral Thermometer		
Adhesive Tape		
Antibiotic Ointment		
Antihistamines		
Crepe Bandages		
Hydrocortisone		
Painkillers		
Safety Pins		
CPR Mouthpiece		
Alcohol Wipes		
Aspirin		
Calamine Lotion		
Splint		
Sterile Eye Dressings		
Medications		
Bandana/Wraps		
First Aid Manual		

4-DAY CAMPING MEAL PLANNER

Great meals make great camping! However, preparing and cooking meals outdoors requires accurate planning to have the right ingredients and equipment for culinary success. Here is a basic meal planning guide for each meal, ingredients, cooking equipment / methods, and grocery list items. Write "Travel" for meals not needed. Use 2 Sheets For 5+Days.

	MEALS	TYPE OF MEAL/FOOD	COOKING METHOD	GROCERY ITEMS/LIST	✓
	Example	Sandwiches / Chips / Fruits	SK/None	Bread, Cold Cuts, Chips, Fruits	✓
DAY 1	Breakfast				
	Snack				
	Lunch				
	Snack				
	Dinner				
	Treat				
DAY 2	Breakfast				
	Snack				
	Lunch				
	Snack				
	Dinner				
	Treat				
DAY 3	Breakfast				
	Snack				
	Lunch				
	Snack				
	Dinner				
	Treat				
DAY 4	Breakfast				
	Snack				
	Lunch				
	Snack				
	Dinner				
	Treat				

*Cooking Methods: (S) Stove   **(G)** Grill   **(F)** Firepit   **(D)** Dutch Oven   **(H)** Hanging Pot   **(Sk)** Skillet

Drinks   ☐ Milk   ☐ Soda   ☐ Tea   ☐ Coffee   ☐ Drink Mix

Spices	**Condiments**	**Fruit**	**Nuts/Mix**	**Fixings**
☐ Salt	☐ Ketchup	☐ Apples	☐ Nuts/Seeds	☐ Lettuce
☐ Pepper	☐ Mustard	☐ Bananas	☐ Trail Mix	☐ Tomatoes
☐ Sugar	☐ Relish	☐ Oranges	☐ Power Bars	☐ Pickes
☐ Hot Sauce	☐ Salsa	☐ Grapefruit	☐ Fruit Bars	☐ Onions
☐ _____	☐ _____	☐ _____	☐ _____	☐ _____

POST-TRIP REVIEW

To make every camping trip better, it's important to capture and review what you liked and what you would change. Use this sheet to review and plan your next adventure.

Campground Name _____ Dates _____ To _____

Address Street _____ City _____ State _____

Type of Site/Park ☐ National ☐ State ☐ Private Campsite # _____

Types of Campsite ☐ Managed/RV ☐ Primitive ☐ Boondocking ☐ Wilderness

Types of Trip ☐ Basic Camping ☐ Glamping (Tent/Rental/RV)
☐ Bushcraft ☐ Primitive ☐ Combination

Sites/Excursions Along the Way

1 _____ 2 _____ 3 _____

Designated Tent / Pad Sites? ☐ Yes ☐ No Campsite # _____

Campground Amenities

☐ Drinking Water (close/far)   ☐ Picnic   ☐ Firewood For Sale
☐ Fire Pits/Ring   ☐ Table – RV (120V 50A/30A)   ☐ Pet Friendly
☐ Tent Pads   ☐ Hookups   ☐ Nice Town
☐ BBQ Grill   ☐ Campground Store

What You Liked / What Went Well?

1 _____

2 _____

Other _____ Restrooms: Yes / No – Close / Far – Clean / Unclean – Shower / Electricity

What You Didn't Like / What Would You Change?

1 _____

2 _____

Animal Sightings _____

Biggest Surprise OR Need That The Campground Had (Or Didn't Have)?_____

Types of Activities Did You Do? (In Tent, Campsite, Campground, Local Areas, etc.)

_____

Things (activities / side trips) To Do Next Time?

_____

People You Met?

Name _____ From City/State _____ Phone/Email _____
Name _____ From City/State _____ Phone/Email _____
Name _____ From City/State _____ Phone/Email _____

TRIP EXPERIENCES

Notes

_____

_____

_____

_____

_____

CAMPING TRIP PLANNING

Ready for your next great outdoor adventure? Use this worksheet to plan your trip and have the greatest "under the stars" experience possible.

What type of trip?

☐ Camping
☐ Tent Glamping
☐ Bushcraft
☐ Backpacking
☐ Combination

Why are you going?

☐ Fun
☐ Activities
☐ Alone Time
☐ Relaxation
☐ Develop and Test New Skills
☐ Others
_____

When will you go on your trip? Dates _____ to _____

Season _____ Seasonal Concerns _____

Location

City _____ ST _____ Park Name _____

Reservations Required?   ☐ Yes ☐ No   ☐ Phone ☐ Web

Reservation # _____

Who is going? Name(s)

_____   _____
_____   _____

New Camping Skills and Preparation (Pitching Tent, Shelter Building, Fire Starting, Cooking, Hunting, Scavenging, Trapping, etc.) **Preparation** (Read, videos, testing, training, certification, etc.)

• Skill _____ How will you prep/test? _____
• Skill _____ How will you prep/test? _____

Special Gear/Equipment (New Type of Tent, Gas Equipment, Generator, Backpacks, Hunting, etc.)

1 _____   2 _____   3 _____

Gear to be purchased, rented or repaired?

1. Type of Gear _____ Purchase, rented, repaired? _____
2. Type of Gear _____ Purchase, rented, repaired? _____

How are you prepared for rain, cold, heat, wind, bugs and varmints?

Rain _____   Cold/Heat _____
Bugs _____   Varmints/Bears _____

Major Activities – What are the different activities you will do?

	Activity	Location
Day 1	_____	_____
Day 2	_____	_____
Day 3	_____	_____
Day 4	_____	_____

Nearest Emergency Room or Help

Facility_____ Address _____ Phone _____ Hours _____

Who Knows You're Gone   Name _____ Phone _____ Email _____

GEAR AND EQUIPMENT CHECKLIST

This is a basic checklist for camping, glamping & bushcraft trips. There are categories and specific camping items. Put an "X" or number in the "#" column in red or blue ink. If you don't want to take an item, then strike through it (e.g. ~~Hammock~~). Once you've loaded an item, mark an X in the LD (Loaded) column. Blanks are for add-ons. **Bolded italicized** items are Bushcraft suggested.

Trip to _____   # Days _____

Trip Type   ☐ Camp   ☐ Glamp   ☐ Bushcraft   Dates _____

Tent/Shelter	#	LD
Tent/Hammock		
Rainfly		
Tent carpet		
Groundsheet/Tarp		
Guy Lines/Stakes		
Mallet/Hammer		
Tent Repair Kit		
Broom/Dustpan		
Sleeping system		
Sleeping Bag		
Sleeping Pad		
Blanket		
Pillow		
Inside/Outside Rug		
Sleeping Cot		
Tent Fan/Heater		
Camp Equipment		
Shelter/Canopy		
Chair		
Table		
Gear		
Backpack/Bag		
Gear Bag		
Knife/Multi-Tool		
Shovel		
Rope		
Strap/Bungee Cords		
Compass		
First Aid Kit		
Saw/Hatchet/Ax		
Duct Tape		
Work Gloves		
Activities		
Hiking/Biking Gear		

Kitchen/Cooking	#	LD
Canopy/Tarp		
Camp Kitchen		
Portable Grill/Grate		
Gas/Electric Stove & Fuel		
Dutch Oven & DO Lifter		
Pots / Pans / Skillet		
Cooler		
Table		
Water Jug		
Trash Can & Bags		
Drink/Coffee Cups		
Charcoal & Starter		
Dish/Biodegradable Soap		
Clothe & Paper Towels		
Grill Utensils/Oven Mitt		
Pots/Dishes		
Mess Kit		
Aluminum Foil		
Big Cutting Knives		
Frying Pan/Spatula		
Coffee Pot/Press/Maker		
Bottle/Wine Opener		
Wipes		
Ice		
Campfire		
Local Firewood		
Matches/Lighter/Starter		
Fire Extinguisher		
Roasting Sticks		
Electrical		
Flashlight		
*Headlamp/*Floodlight		
Lantern Fuel/Electric		
Extension Cord		
Extra Batteries / Charger		
Activities		
Fishing Gear / Bait		

Personal	#	LD
GUYS		
Jacket/Coat		
Shirts		
Pants		
Shorts		
Underwear		
Hygiene Kit		
Hat / Visor		
Socks		
Shoes / Boots		
Rain Gear		
Swimwear		
Sleepwear		
GIRLS		
Jacket/Coat		
Shirts/Blouses		
Pants		
Shorts		
Underwear		
Hygiene Kit		
Hat/Visor		
Socks		
Shoes/Boots		
Rain Gear		
Swimwear		
Sleepwear		
Misc		
Sunscreen/Bug Spray		
Bath Cloth/Towels		
Sunglasses		
Bandana		
Binoculars		
Activities		
Board Games/Cards		

PERSONAL ITEMS / FIRST AID

This checklist is for packing personal items for hygiene, miscellaneous, and first aid. The personal item section is designed for 4 people. To add more adults or children, just make a line to the right of the item. Use blank spaces for additional items.

Personal Item	Camper #1 ✓	#	Camper #2 ✓	#	Camper #3 ✓	#	Camper #4 ✓	#
Soap								
Toothbrush								
Toothpaste								
Dental Floss								
Deodorant								
Shampoo/Conditioner								
Comb/Brush								
Tissues								
Razor								
Shaving Cream								
Hand Sanitizer								
Cotton Tips								
Lotion								
Mouthwash								
Dental Floss								
Chapstick/Lip Balm								
Toilet Paper								
Tweezers								
Sunscreen								
Insect Repellent								
Washcloth								
Towel								
Mirror								
Hair Dryer								
Contacts/Case								
Saline Solution								
Nail Clippers/File								
Ear Plugs								
Medications								

First Aid Kit Checklist

First Aid Item	✓	#
Band Aids		
Gauze Pads		
Antiseptic Wipes		
Hydrogen Peroxide		
Cotton Balls		
Sanitizer		
Tweezers		
Scissors		
Instant Cold/Hot Packs		
Latex Gloves		
Blanket		
Oral Thermometer		
Adhesive Tape		
Antibiotic Ointment		
Antihistamines		
Crepe Bandages		
Hydrocortisone		
Painkillers		
Safety Pins		
CPR Mouthpiece		
Alcohol Wipes		
Aspirin		
Calamine Lotion		
Splint		
Sterile Eye Dressings		
Medications		
Bandana/Wraps		
First Aid Manual		

4-DAY CAMPING MEAL PLANNER

Great meals make great camping! However, preparing and cooking meals outdoors requires accurate planning to have the right ingredients and equipment for culinary success. Here is a basic meal planning guide for each meal, ingredients, cooking equipment / methods, and grocery list items. Write "Travel" for meals not needed. Use 2 Sheets For 5+Days.

	MEALS	TYPE OF MEAL/FOOD	COOKING METHOD	GROCERY ITEMS/LIST	✓
	Example	Sandwiches / Chips / Fruits	SK/None	Bread, Cold Cuts, Chips, Fruits	✓
DAY 1	Breakfast				
	Snack				
	Lunch				
	Snack				
	Dinner				
	Treat				
DAY 2	Breakfast				
	Snack				
	Lunch				
	Snack				
	Dinner				
	Treat				
DAY 3	Breakfast				
	Snack				
	Lunch				
	Snack				
	Dinner				
	Treat				
DAY 4	Breakfast				
	Snack				
	Lunch				
	Snack				
	Dinner				
	Treat				

*Cooking Methods: (S) Stove **(G)** Grill **(F)** Firepit **(D)** Dutch Oven **(H)** Hanging Pot **(Sk)** Skillet

Drinks ☐ Milk ☐ Soda ☐ Tea ☐ Coffee ☐ Drink Mix

Spices	**Condiments**	**Fruit**	**Nuts/Mix**	**Fixings**
☐ Salt	☐ Ketchup	☐ Apples	☐ Nuts/Seeds	☐ Lettuce
☐ Pepper	☐ Mustard	☐ Bananas	☐ Trail Mix	☐ Tomatoes
☐ Sugar	☐ Relish	☐ Oranges	☐ Power Bars	☐ Pickes
☐ Hot Sauce	☐ Salsa	☐ Grapefruit	☐ Fruit Bars	☐ Onions
☐ _____	☐ _____	☐ _____	☐ _____	☐ _____

POST-TRIP REVIEW

To make every camping trip better, it's important to capture and review what you liked and what you would change. Use this sheet to review and plan your next adventure.

Campground Name _____ Dates _____ To _____

Address Street _____ City _____ State _____

Type of Site/Park ☐ National ☐ State ☐ Private Campsite # _____

Types of Campsite ☐ Managed/RV ☐ Primitive ☐ Boondocking ☐ Wilderness

Types of Trip ☐ Basic Camping ☐ Glamping (Tent/Rental/RV)
☐ Bushcraft ☐ Primitive ☐ Combination

Sites/Excursions Along the Way

1 _____ 2 _____ 3 _____

Designated Tent / Pad Sites? ☐ Yes ☐ No Campsite # _____

Campground Amenities

☐ Drinking Water (close/far)   ☐ Picnic   ☐ Firewood For Sale
☐ Fire Pits/Ring   ☐ Table – RV (120V 50A/30A)   ☐ Pet Friendly
☐ Tent Pads   ☐ Hookups   ☐ Nice Town
☐ BBQ Grill   ☐ Campground Store

What You Liked / What Went Well?

1 _____

2 _____

Other _____ Restrooms: Yes / No – Close / Far – Clean / Unclean – Shower / Electricity

What You Didn't Like / What Would You Change?

1 _____

2 _____

Animal Sightings _____

Biggest Surprise OR Need That The Campground Had (Or Didn't Have)? _____

Types of Activities Did You Do? (In Tent, Campsite, Campground, Local Areas, etc.)

_____

Things (activities / side trips) To Do Next Time?

_____

People You Met?

Name _____ From City/State _____ Phone/Email _____
Name _____ From City/State _____ Phone/Email _____
Name _____ From City/State _____ Phone/Email _____

TRIP EXPERIENCES

PICTURES · MEMORIES · MAPS · MISC. · NOTES

Notes

_____

_____

_____

_____

CAMPING TRIP PLANNING

Ready for your next great outdoor adventure? Use this worksheet to plan your trip and have the greatest "under the stars" experience possible.

What type of trip?

☐ Camping
☐ Tent Glamping
☐ Bushcraft
☐ Backpacking
☐ Combination

Why are you going?

☐ Fun
☐ Activities
☐ Alone Time
☐ Relaxation
☐ Develop and Test New Skills
☐ Others
_____

When will you go on your trip? Dates _____ to _____

Season _____ Seasonal Concerns _____

Location

City _____ ST _____ Park Name _____

Reservations Required? ☐ Yes ☐ No   ☐ Phone ☐ Web

Reservation # _____

Who is going? Name(s)

_____ _____
_____ _____

New Camping Skills and Preparation (Pitching Tent, Shelter Building, Fire Starting, Cooking, Hunting, Scavenging, Trapping, etc.) **Preparation** (Read, videos, testing, training, certification, etc.)

- Skill _____ How will you prep/test? _____
- Skill _____ How will you prep/test? _____

Special Gear/Equipment (New Type of Tent, Gas Equipment, Generator, Backpacks, Hunting, etc.)

1 _____   2 _____   3 _____

Gear to be purchased, rented or repaired?

1. Type of Gear _____ Purchase, rented, repaired? _____
2. Type of Gear _____ Purchase, rented, repaired? _____

How are you prepared for rain, cold, heat, wind, bugs and varmints?

Rain _____   Cold/Heat _____
Bugs _____   Varmints/Bears _____

Major Activities – What are the different activities you will do?

	Activity	Location
Day 1	_____	_____
Day 2	_____	_____
Day 3	_____	_____
Day 4	_____	_____

Nearest Emergency Room or Help

Facility_____ Address _____ Phone _____ Hours _____

Who Knows You're Gone   Name _____ Phone _____ Email _____

GEAR AND EQUIPMENT CHECKLIST

This is a basic checklist for camping, glamping & bushcraft trips. There are categories and specific camping items. Put an "X" or number in the "#" column in red or blue ink. If you don't want to take an item, then strike through it (e.g. ~~Hammock~~). Once you've loaded an item, mark an X in the LD (Loaded) column. Blanks are for add-ons. **Bolded italicized** items are Bushcraft suggested.

Trip to _____ # Days _____

Trip Type ☐ Camp   ☐ Glamp   ☐ Bushcraft   Dates _____

Tent/Shelter	#	LD
Tent/Hammock		
Rainfly		
Tent carpet		
Groundsheet/Tarp		
Guy Lines/Stakes		
Mallet/Hammer		
Tent Repair Kit		
Broom/Dustpan		
Sleeping system		
Sleeping Bag		
Sleeping Pad		
Blanket		
Pillow		
Inside/Outside Rug		
Sleeping Cot		
Tent Fan/Heater		
Camp Equipment		
Shelter/Canopy		
Chair		
Table		
Gear		
Backpack/Bag		
Gear Bag		
Knife/Multi-Tool		
Shovel		
Rope		
Strap/Bungee Cords		
Compass		
First Aid Kit		
Saw/Hatchet/Ax		
Duct Tape		
Work Gloves		
Activities		
Hiking/Biking Gear		

Kitchen/Cooking	#	LD
Canopy/Tarp		
Camp Kitchen		
Portable Grill/Grate		
Gas/Electric Stove & Fuel		
Dutch Oven & DO Lifter		
Pots / Pans / Skillet		
Cooler		
Table		
Water Jug		
Trash Can & Bags		
Drink/Coffee Cups		
Charcoal & Starter		
Dish/Biodegradable Soap		
Clothe & Paper Towels		
Grill Utensils/Oven Mitt		
Pots/Dishes		
Mess Kit		
Aluminum Foil		
Big Cutting Knives		
Frying Pan/Spatula		
Coffee Pot/Press/Maker		
Bottle/Wine Opener		
Wipes		
Ice		
Campfire		
Local Firewood		
Matches/Lighter/Starter		
Fire Extinguisher		
Roasting Sticks		
Electrical		
Flashlight		
*Headlamp/*Floodlight		
Lantern Fuel/Electric		
Extension Cord		
Extra Batteries / Charger		
Activities		
Fishing Gear / Bait		

Personal	#	LD
GUYS		
Jacket/Coat		
Shirts		
Pants		
Shorts		
Underwear		
Hygiene Kit		
Hat / Visor		
Socks		
Shoes / Boots		
Rain Gear		
Swimwear		
Sleepwear		
GIRLS		
Jacket/Coat		
Shirts/Blouses		
Pants		
Shorts		
Underwear		
Hygiene Kit		
Hat/Visor		
Socks		
Shoes/Boots		
Rain Gear		
Swimwear		
Sleepwear		
Misc		
Sunscreen/Bug Spray		
Bath Cloth/Towels		
Sunglasses		
Bandana		
Binoculars		
Activities		
Board Games/Cards		

PERSONAL ITEMS / FIRST AID

This checklist is for packing personal items for hygiene, miscellaneous, and first aid. The personal item section is designed for 4 people. To add more adults or children, just make a line to the right of the item. Use blank spaces for additional items.

Personal Item	Camper #1 ✓ | #	Camper #2 ✓ | #	Camper #3 ✓ | #	Camper #4 ✓ | #
Soap				
Toothbrush				
Toothpaste				
Dental Floss				
Deodorant				
Shampoo/Conditioner				
Comb/Brush				
Tissues				
Razor				
Shaving Cream				
Hand Sanitizer				
Cotton Tips				
Lotion				
Mouthwash				
Dental Floss				
Chapstick/Lip Balm				
Toilet Paper				
Tweezers				
Sunscreen				
Insect Repellent				
Washcloth				
Towel				
Mirror				
Hair Dryer				
Contacts/Case				
Saline Solution				
Nail Clippers/File				
Ear Plugs				
Medications				

First Aid Kit Checklist

First Aid Item	✓ | #
Band Aids	
Gauze Pads	
Antiseptic Wipes	
Hydrogen Peroxide	
Cotton Balls	
Sanitizer	
Tweezers	
Scissors	
Instant Cold/Hot Packs	
Latex Gloves	
Blanket	
Oral Thermometer	
Adhesive Tape	
Antibiotic Ointment	
Antihistamines	
Crepe Bandages	
Hydrocortisone	
Painkillers	
Safety Pins	
CPR Mouthpiece	
Alcohol Wipes	
Aspirin	
Calamine Lotion	
Splint	
Sterile Eye Dressings	
Medications	
Bandana/Wraps	
First Aid Manual	

4-DAY CAMPING MEAL PLANNER

Great meals make great camping! However, preparing and cooking meals outdoors requires accurate planning to have the right ingredients and equipment for culinary success. Here is a basic meal planning guide for each meal, ingredients, cooking equipment / methods, and grocery list items. Write "Travel" for meals not needed. Use 2 Sheets For 5+Days.

	MEALS	TYPE OF MEAL/FOOD	COOKING METHOD	GROCERY ITEMS/LIST	✓
	Example	Sandwiches / Chips / Fruits	SK/None	Bread, Cold Cuts, Chips, Fruits	✓
DAY 1	Breakfast				
	Snack				
	Lunch				
	Snack				
	Dinner				
	Treat				
DAY 2	Breakfast				
	Snack				
	Lunch				
	Snack				
	Dinner				
	Treat				
DAY 3	Breakfast				
	Snack				
	Lunch				
	Snack				
	Dinner				
	Treat				
DAY 4	Breakfast				
	Snack				
	Lunch				
	Snack				
	Dinner				
	Treat				

*Cooking Methods: **(S)** Stove **(G)** Grill **(F)** Firepit **(D)** Dutch Oven **(H)** Hanging Pot **(Sk)** Skillet

Drinks   ☐ Milk   ☐ Soda   ☐ Tea   ☐ Coffee   ☐ Drink Mix

Spices	**Condiments**	**Fruit**	**Nuts/Mix**	**Fixings**
☐ Salt	☐ Ketchup	☐ Apples	☐ Nuts/Seeds	☐ Lettuce
☐ Pepper	☐ Mustard	☐ Bananas	☐ Trail Mix	☐ Tomatoes
☐ Sugar	☐ Relish	☐ Oranges	☐ Power Bars	☐ Pickes
☐ Hot Sauce	☐ Salsa	☐ Grapefruit	☐ Fruit Bars	☐ Onions
☐ _____	☐ _____	☐ _____	☐ _____	☐ _____

POST-TRIP REVIEW

To make every camping trip better, it's important to capture and review what you liked and what you would change. Use this sheet to review and plan your next adventure.

Campground Name _____ Dates _____ To _____

Address Street _____ City _____ State _____

Type of Site/Park ☐ National   ☐ State   ☐ Private   Campsite # _____

Types of Campsite ☐ Managed/RV   ☐ Primitive   ☐ Boondocking   ☐ Wilderness

Types of Trip ☐ Basic Camping   ☐ Glamping (Tent/Rental/RV)
☐ Bushcraft   ☐ Primitive   ☐ Combination

Sites/Excursions Along the Way

1 _____ 2 _____ 3 _____

Designated Tent / Pad Sites?   ☐ Yes   ☐ No   Campsite # _____

Campground Amenities

☐ Drinking Water (close/far)   ☐ Picnic   ☐ Firewood For Sale
☐ Fire Pits/Ring   ☐ Table – RV (120V 50A/30A)   ☐ Pet Friendly
☐ Tent Pads   ☐ Hookups   ☐ Nice Town
☐ BBQ Grill   ☐ Campground Store

What You Liked / What Went Well?

1 _____

2 _____

Other _____ Restrooms: Yes / No – Close / Far – Clean / Unclean – Shower / Electricity

What You Didn't Like / What Would You Change?

1 _____

2 _____

Animal Sightings _____

Biggest Surprise OR Need That The Campground Had (Or Didn't Have)?_____

Types of Activities Did You Do? (In Tent, Campsite, Campground, Local Areas, etc.)

_____

Things (activities / side trips) To Do Next Time?

_____

People You Met?

Name _____ From City/State _____ Phone/Email _____
Name _____ From City/State _____ Phone/Email _____
Name _____ From City/State _____ Phone/Email _____

TRIP EXPERIENCES

Notes

_____

_____

_____

_____

_____

CAMPING TRIP PLANNING

Ready for your next great outdoor adventure? Use this worksheet to plan your trip and have the greatest "under the stars" experience possible.

What type of trip?

- ☐ Camping
- ☐ Tent Glamping
- ☐ Bushcraft
- ☐ Backpacking
- ☐ Combination

Why are you going?

- ☐ Fun
- ☐ Activities
- ☐ Alone Time
- ☐ Relaxation
- ☐ Develop and Test New Skills
- ☐ Others
  _____

When will you go on your trip? Dates _____ to _____

Season _____   Seasonal Concerns _____

Location

City _____   ST _____   Park Name _____

Reservations Required?   ☐ Yes ☐ No   ☐ Phone ☐ Web

Reservation # _____

Who is going? Name(s)

_____   _____
_____   _____

New Camping Skills and Preparation (Pitching Tent, Shelter Building, Fire Starting, Cooking, Hunting, Scavenging, Trapping, etc.) **Preparation** (Read, videos, testing, training, certification, etc.)

- Skill _____ How will you prep/test? _____
- Skill _____ How will you prep/test? _____

Special Gear/Equipment (New Type of Tent, Gas Equipment, Generator, Backpacks, Hunting, etc.)

1 _____   2 _____   3 _____

Gear to be purchased, rented or repaired?

1. Type of Gear _____ Purchase, rented, repaired? _____
2. Type of Gear _____ Purchase, rented, repaired? _____

How are you prepared for rain, cold, heat, wind, bugs and varmints?

Rain _____   Cold/Heat _____

Bugs _____   Varmints/Bears _____

Major Activities – What are the different activities you will do?

	Activity	Location
Day 1	_____	_____
Day 2	_____	_____
Day 3	_____	_____
Day 4	_____	_____

Nearest Emergency Room or Help

Facility_____ Address _____ Phone _____ Hours _____

Who Knows You're Gone   Name _____ Phone _____ Email _____

GEAR AND EQUIPMENT CHECKLIST

This is a basic checklist for camping, glamping & bushcraft trips. There are categories and specific camping items. Put an "X" or number in the "#" column in red or blue ink. If you don't want to take an item, then strike through it (e.g. ~~Hammock~~). Once you've loaded an item, mark an X in the LD (Loaded) column. Blanks are for add-ons. **Bolded italicized** items are Bushcraft suggested.

Trip to _____ # Days _____

Trip Type ☐ Camp   ☐ Glamp   ☐ Bushcraft   Dates _____

Tent/Shelter	#	LD
Tent/Hammock		
Rainfly		
Tent carpet		
Groundsheet/Tarp		
Guy Lines/Stakes		
Mallet/Hammer		
Tent Repair Kit		
Broom/Dustpan		
Sleeping system		
Sleeping Bag		
Sleeping Pad		
Blanket		
Pillow		
Inside/Outside Rug		
Sleeping Cot		
Tent Fan/Heater		
Camp Equipment		
Shelter/Canopy		
Chair		
Table		
Gear		
Backpack/Bag		
Gear Bag		
Knife/Multi-Tool		
Shovel		
Rope		
Strap/Bungee Cords		
Compass		
First Aid Kit		
Saw/Hatchet/Ax		
Duct Tape		
Work Gloves		
Activities		
Hiking/Biking Gear		

Kitchen/Cooking	#	LD
Canopy/Tarp		
Camp Kitchen		
Portable Grill/Grate		
Gas/Electric Stove & Fuel		
Dutch Oven & DO Lifter		
Pots / Pans / Skillet		
Cooler		
Table		
Water Jug		
Trash Can & Bags		
Drink/Coffee Cups		
Charcoal & Starter		
Dish/Biodegradable Soap		
Clothe & Paper Towels		
Grill Utensils/Oven Mitt		
Pots/Dishes		
Mess Kit		
Aluminum Foil		
Big Cutting Knives		
Frying Pan/Spatula		
Coffee Pot/Press/Maker		
Bottle/Wine Opener		
Wipes		
Ice		
Campfire		
Local Firewood		
Matches/Lighter/Starter		
Fire Extinguisher		
Roasting Sticks		
Electrical		
Flashlight		
Headlamp/Floodlight		
Lantern Fuel/Electric		
Extension Cord		
Extra Batteries / Charger		
Activities		
Fishing Gear / Bait		

Personal	#	LD
GUYS		
Jacket/Coat		
Shirts		
Pants		
Shorts		
Underwear		
Hygiene Kit		
Hat / Visor		
Socks		
Shoes / Boots		
Rain Gear		
Swimwear		
Sleepwear		
GIRLS		
Jacket/Coat		
Shirts/Blouses		
Pants		
Shorts		
Underwear		
Hygiene Kit		
Hat/Visor		
Socks		
Shoes/Boots		
Rain Gear		
Swimwear		
Sleepwear		
Misc		
Sunscreen/Bug Spray		
Bath Cloth/Towels		
Sunglasses		
Bandana		
Binoculars		
Activities		
Board Games/Cards		

PERSONAL ITEMS / FIRST AID

This checklist is for packing personal items for hygiene, miscellaneous, and first aid. The personal item section is designed for 4 people. To add more adults or children, just make a line to the right of the item. Use blank spaces for additional items.

Personal Item	Camper #1 ✓ | #	Camper #2 ✓ | #	Camper #3 ✓ | #	Camper #4 ✓ | #
Soap				
Toothbrush				
Toothpaste				
Dental Floss				
Deodorant				
Shampoo/Conditioner				
Comb/Brush				
Tissues				
Razor				
Shaving Cream				
Hand Sanitizer				
Cotton Tips				
Lotion				
Mouthwash				
Dental Floss				
Chapstick/Lip Balm				
Toilet Paper				
Tweezers				
Sunscreen				
Insect Repellent				
Washcloth				
Towel				
Mirror				
Hair Dryer				
Contacts/Case				
Saline Solution				
Nail Clippers/File				
Ear Plugs				
Medications				

First Aid Kit Checklist

First Aid Item	✓ | #
Band Aids	
Gauze Pads	
Antiseptic Wipes	
Hydrogen Peroxide	
Cotton Balls	
Sanitizer	
Tweezers	
Scissors	
Instant Cold/Hot Packs	
Latex Gloves	
Blanket	
Oral Thermometer	
Adhesive Tape	
Antibiotic Ointment	
Antihistamines	
Crepe Bandages	
Hydrocortisone	
Painkillers	
Safety Pins	
CPR Mouthpiece	
Alcohol Wipes	
Aspirin	
Calamine Lotion	
Splint	
Sterile Eye Dressings	
Medications	
Bandana/Wraps	
First Aid Manual	

4-DAY CAMPING MEAL PLANNER

Great meals make great camping! However, preparing and cooking meals outdoors requires accurate planning to have the right ingredients and equipment for culinary success. Here is a basic meal planning guide for each meal, ingredients, cooking equipment / methods, and grocery list items. Write "Travel" for meals not needed. Use 2 Sheets For 5+Days.

	MEALS	TYPE OF MEAL/FOOD	COOKING METHOD	GROCERY ITEMS/LIST	✓
	Example	Sandwiches / Chips / Fruits	SK/None	Bread, Cold Cuts, Chips, Fruits	✓
DAY 1	Breakfast				
	Snack				
	Lunch				
	Snack				
	Dinner				
	Treat				
DAY 2	Breakfast				
	Snack				
	Lunch				
	Snack				
	Dinner				
	Treat				
DAY 3	Breakfast				
	Snack				
	Lunch				
	Snack				
	Dinner				
	Treat				
DAY 4	Breakfast				
	Snack				
	Lunch				
	Snack				
	Dinner				
	Treat				

*Cooking Methods: **(S)** Stove   **(G)** Grill   **(F)** Firepit   **(D)** Dutch Oven   **(H)** Hanging Pot   **(Sk)** Skillet

Drinks   ☐ Milk   ☐ Soda   ☐ Tea   ☐ Coffee   ☐ Drink Mix

Spices	**Condiments**	**Fruit**	**Nuts/Mix**	**Fixings**
☐ Salt	☐ Ketchup	☐ Apples	☐ Nuts/Seeds	☐ Lettuce
☐ Pepper	☐ Mustard	☐ Bananas	☐ Trail Mix	☐ Tomatoes
☐ Sugar	☐ Relish	☐ Oranges	☐ Power Bars	☐ Pickes
☐ Hot Sauce	☐ Salsa	☐ Grapefruit	☐ Fruit Bars	☐ Onions
☐ _____	☐ _____	☐ _____	☐ _____	☐ _____

POST-TRIP REVIEW

To make every camping trip better, it's important to capture and review what you liked and what you would change. Use this sheet to review and plan your next adventure.

Campground Name _____ Dates _____ To _____

Address Street _____ City _____ State _____

Type of Site/Park ☐ National ☐ State ☐ Private Campsite # _____

Types of Campsite ☐ Managed/RV ☐ Primitive ☐ Boondocking ☐ Wilderness

Types of Trip ☐ Basic Camping ☐ Glamping (Tent/Rental/RV)
☐ Bushcraft ☐ Primitive ☐ Combination

Sites/Excursions Along the Way

1 _____ 2 _____ 3 _____

Designated Tent / Pad Sites? ☐ Yes ☐ No Campsite # _____

Campground Amenities

☐ Drinking Water (close/far)   ☐ Picnic   ☐ Firewood For Sale
☐ Fire Pits/Ring   ☐ Table – RV (120V 50A/30A)   ☐ Pet Friendly
☐ Tent Pads   ☐ Hookups   ☐ Nice Town
☐ BBQ Grill   ☐ Campground Store

What You Liked / What Went Well?

1 _____

2 _____

Other _____ Restrooms: Yes / No – Close / Far – Clean / Unclean – Shower / Electricity

What You Didn't Like / What Would You Change?

1 _____

2 _____

Animal Sightings _____

Biggest Surprise OR Need That The Campground Had (Or Didn't Have)?_____

Types of Activities Did You Do? (In Tent, Campsite, Campground, Local Areas, etc.)

_____

Things (activities / side trips) To Do Next Time?

_____

People You Met?

Name _____ From City/State _____ Phone/Email _____
Name _____ From City/State _____ Phone/Email _____
Name _____ From City/State _____ Phone/Email _____

Notes

_____

_____

_____

_____

CAMPING TRIP PLANNING

What type of trip?

☐ Camping
☐ Tent Glamping
☐ Bushcraft
☐ Backpacking
☐ Combination

Why are you going?

☐ Fun
☐ Activities
☐ Alone Time
☐ Relaxation
☐ Develop and Test New Skills
☐ Others
_____

When will you go on your trip? Dates _____ to _____

Season _____ Seasonal Concerns _____

Location

City _____ ST _____ Park Name _____

Reservations Required? ☐ Yes ☐ No   ☐ Phone ☐ Web

Reservation # _____

Who is going? Name(s)

_____   _____
_____   _____

New Camping Skills and Preparation (Pitching Tent, Shelter Building, Fire Starting, Cooking, Hunting, Scavenging, Trapping, etc.) **Preparation** (Read, videos, testing, training, certification, etc.)

• Skill _____ How will you prep/test? _____
• Skill _____ How will you prep/test? _____

Special Gear/Equipment (New Type of Tent, Gas Equipment, Generator, Backpacks, Hunting, etc.)

1 _____   2 _____   3 _____

Gear to be purchased, rented or repaired?

1. Type of Gear _____ Purchase, rented, repaired? _____
2. Type of Gear _____ Purchase, rented, repaired? _____

How are you prepared for rain, cold, heat, wind, bugs and varmints?

Rain _____   Cold/Heat _____
Bugs _____   Varmints/Bears _____

Major Activities – What are the different activities you will do?

	Activity	Location
Day 1	_____	_____
Day 2	_____	_____
Day 3	_____	_____
Day 4	_____	_____

Nearest Emergency Room or Help

Facility_____ Address _____ Phone _____ Hours _____

Who Knows You're Gone Name _____ Phone _____ Email _____

GEAR AND EQUIPMENT CHECKLIST

This is a basic checklist for camping, glamping & bushcraft trips. There are categories and specific camping items. Put an "X" or number in the "#" column in red or blue ink. If you don't want to take an item, then strike through it (e.g. ~~Hammock~~). Once you've loaded an item, mark an X in the LD (Loaded) column. Blanks are for add-ons. **Bolded italicized** items are Bushcraft suggested.

Trip to _____   # Days _____

Trip Type   ☐ Camp   ☐ Glamp   ☐ Bushcraft   Dates _____

Tent/Shelter	#	LD
Tent/Hammock		
Rainfly		
Tent carpet		
Groundsheet/Tarp		
Guy Lines/Stakes		
Mallet/Hammer		
Tent Repair Kit		
Broom/Dustpan		
Sleeping system		
Sleeping Bag		
Sleeping Pad		
Blanket		
Pillow		
Inside/Outside Rug		
Sleeping Cot		
Tent Fan/Heater		
Camp Equipment		
Shelter/Canopy		
Chair		
Table		
Gear		
Backpack/Bag		
Gear Bag		
Knife/Multi-Tool		
Shovel		
Rope		
Strap/Bungee Cords		
Compass		
First Aid Kit		
Saw/Hatchet/Ax		
Duct Tape		
Work Gloves		
Activities		
Hiking/Biking Gear		

Kitchen/Cooking	#	LD
Canopy/Tarp		
Camp Kitchen		
Portable Grill/Grate		
Gas/Electric Stove & Fuel		
Dutch Oven & DO Lifter		
Pots / Pans / Skillet		
Cooler		
Table		
Water Jug		
Trash Can & Bags		
Drink/Coffee Cups		
Charcoal & Starter		
Dish/Biodegradable Soap		
Clothe & Paper Towels		
Grill Utensils/Oven Mitt		
Pots/Dishes		
Mess Kit		
Aluminum Foil		
Big Cutting Knives		
Frying Pan/Spatula		
Coffee Pot/Press/Maker		
Bottle/Wine Opener		
Wipes		
Ice		
Campfire		
Local Firewood		
Matches/Lighter/Starter		
Fire Extinguisher		
Roasting Sticks		
Electrical		
Flashlight		
Headlamp/Floodlight		
Lantern Fuel/Electric		
Extension Cord		
Extra Batteries / Charger		
Activities		
Fishing Gear / Bait		

Personal	#	LD
GUYS		
Jacket/Coat		
Shirts		
Pants		
Shorts		
Underwear		
Hygiene Kit		
Hat / Visor		
Socks		
Shoes / Boots		
Rain Gear		
Swimwear		
Sleepwear		
GIRLS		
Jacket/Coat		
Shirts/Blouses		
Pants		
Shorts		
Underwear		
Hygiene Kit		
Hat/Visor		
Socks		
Shoes/Boots		
Rain Gear		
Swimwear		
Sleepwear		
Misc		
Sunscreen/Bug Spray		
Bath Cloth/Towels		
Sunglasses		
Bandana		
Binoculars		
Activities		
Board Games/Cards		

PERSONAL ITEMS / FIRST AID

This checklist is for packing personal items for hygiene, miscellaneous, and first aid. The personal item section is designed for 4 people. To add more adults or children, just make a line to the right of the item. Use blank spaces for additional items.

Personal Item	Camper #1 ✓ | #	Camper #2 ✓ | #	Camper #3 ✓ | #	Camper #4 ✓ | #
Soap				
Toothbrush				
Toothpaste				
Dental Floss				
Deodorant				
Shampoo/Conditioner				
Comb/Brush				
Tissues				
Razor				
Shaving Cream				
Hand Sanitizer				
Cotton Tips				
Lotion				
Mouthwash				
Dental Floss				
Chapstick/Lip Balm				
Toilet Paper				
Tweezers				
Sunscreen				
Insect Repellent				
Washcloth				
Towel				
Mirror				
Hair Dryer				
Contacts/Case				
Saline Solution				
Nail Clippers/File				
Ear Plugs				
Medications				

First Aid Kit Checklist

First Aid Item	✓ | #
Band Aids	
Gauze Pads	
Antiseptic Wipes	
Hydrogen Peroxide	
Cotton Balls	
Sanitizer	
Tweezers	
Scissors	
Instant Cold/Hot Packs	
Latex Gloves	
Blanket	
Oral Thermometer	
Adhesive Tape	
Antibiotic Ointment	
Antihistamines	
Crepe Bandages	
Hydrocortisone	
Painkillers	
Safety Pins	
CPR Mouthpiece	
Alcohol Wipes	
Aspirin	
Calamine Lotion	
Splint	
Sterile Eye Dressings	
Medications	
Bandana/Wraps	
First Aid Manual	

4-DAY CAMPING MEAL PLANNER

Great meals make great camping! However, preparing and cooking meals outdoors requires accurate planning to have the right ingredients and equipment for culinary success. Here is a basic meal planning guide for each meal, ingredients, cooking equipment / methods, and grocery list items. Write "Travel" for meals not needed. Use 2 Sheets For 5+Days.

MEALS	TYPE OF MEAL/FOOD	COOKING METHOD	GROCERY ITEMS/LIST	✓
Example	Sandwiches / Chips / Fruits	SK/None	Bread, Cold Cuts, Chips, Fruits	✓
DAY 1 Breakfast				
Snack				
Lunch				
Snack				
Dinner				
Treat				
DAY 2 Breakfast				
Snack				
Lunch				
Snack				
Dinner				
Treat				
DAY 3 Breakfast				
Snack				
Lunch				
Snack				
Dinner				
Treat				
DAY 4 Breakfast				
Snack				
Lunch				
Snack				
Dinner				
Treat				

*Cooking Methods: **(S)** Stove **(G)** Grill **(F)** Firepit **(D)** Dutch Oven **(H)** Hanging Pot **(Sk)** Skillet

Drinks ☐ Milk ☐ Soda ☐ Tea ☐ Coffee ☐ Drink Mix

Spices	**Condiments**	**Fruit**	**Nuts/Mix**	**Fixings**
☐ Salt	☐ Ketchup	☐ Apples	☐ Nuts/Seeds	☐ Lettuce
☐ Pepper	☐ Mustard	☐ Bananas	☐ Trail Mix	☐ Tomatoes
☐ Sugar	☐ Relish	☐ Oranges	☐ Power Bars	☐ Pickes
☐ Hot Sauce	☐ Salsa	☐ Grapefruit	☐ Fruit Bars	☐ Onions
☐ _____	☐ _____	☐ _____	☐ _____	☐ _____

POST-TRIP REVIEW

To make every camping trip better, it's important to capture and review what you liked and what you would change. Use this sheet to review and plan your next adventure.

Campground Name _____ Dates _____ To _____

Address Street _____ City _____ State _____

Type of Site/Park ☐ National ☐ State ☐ Private Campsite # _____

Types of Campsite ☐ Managed/RV ☐ Primitive ☐ Boondocking ☐ Wilderness

Types of Trip ☐ Basic Camping ☐ Glamping (Tent/Rental/RV)
☐ Bushcraft ☐ Primitive ☐ Combination

Sites/Excursions Along the Way

1 _____ 2 _____ 3 _____

Designated Tent / Pad Sites? ☐ Yes ☐ No Campsite # _____

Campground Amenities

☐ Drinking Water (close/far)   ☐ Picnic   ☐ Firewood For Sale
☐ Fire Pits/Ring   ☐ Table – RV (120V 50A/30A)   ☐ Pet Friendly
☐ Tent Pads   ☐ Hookups   ☐ Nice Town
☐ BBQ Grill   ☐ Campground Store

What You Liked / What Went Well?

1 _____

2 _____

Other _____ Restrooms: Yes / No – Close / Far – Clean / Unclean – Shower / Electricity

What You Didn't Like / What Would You Change?

1 _____

2 _____

Animal Sightings _____

Biggest Surprise OR Need That The Campground Had (Or Didn't Have)?_____

Types of Activities Did You Do? (In Tent, Campsite, Campground, Local Areas, etc.)

_____

Things (activities / side trips) To Do Next Time?

_____

People You Met?

Name _____ From City/State _____ Phone/Email _____
Name _____ From City/State _____ Phone/Email _____
Name _____ From City/State _____ Phone/Email _____

TRIP EXPERIENCES

Notes

CAMPING TRIP PLANNING

Ready for your next great outdoor adventure? Use this worksheet to plan your trip and have the greatest "under the stars" experience possible.

What type of trip?

☐ Camping
☐ Tent Glamping
☐ Bushcraft
☐ Backpacking
☐ Combination

Why are you going?

☐ Fun
☐ Activities
☐ Alone Time
☐ Relaxation
☐ Develop and
   Test New Skills
☐ Others
_____

When will you go on your trip? Dates _____ to _____

Season _____ Seasonal Concerns _____

Location

City _____ ST _____ Park Name _____

Reservations Required? ☐ Yes ☐ No   ☐ Phone ☐ Web

Reservation # _____

Who is going? Name(s)

_____ _____
_____ _____

New Camping Skills and Preparation (Pitching Tent, Shelter Building, Fire Starting, Cooking, Hunting, Scavenging, Trapping, etc.) **Preparation** (Read, videos, testing, training, certification, etc.)

- Skill _____ How will you prep/test? _____
- Skill _____ How will you prep/test? _____

Special Gear/Equipment (New Type of Tent, Gas Equipment, Generator, Backpacks, Hunting, etc.)

1 _____   2 _____   3 _____

Gear to be purchased, rented or repaired?

1. Type of Gear _____ Purchase, rented, repaired? _____
2. Type of Gear _____ Purchase, rented, repaired? _____

How are you prepared for rain, cold, heat, wind, bugs and varmints?

Rain _____   Cold/Heat _____
Bugs _____   Varmints/Bears _____

Major Activities – What are the different activities you will do?

	Activity	Location
Day 1	_____	_____
Day 2	_____	_____
Day 3	_____	_____
Day 4	_____	_____

Nearest Emergency Room or Help

Facility_____ Address _____ Phone _____ Hours _____

Who Knows You're Gone Name _____ Phone _____ Email _____

GEAR AND EQUIPMENT CHECKLIST

This is a basic checklist for camping, glamping & bushcraft trips. There are categories and specific camping items. Put an "X" or number in the "#" column in red or blue ink. If you don't want to take an item, then strike through it (e.g. ~~Hammock~~). Once you've loaded an item, mark an X in the LD (Loaded) column. Blanks are for add-ons. **Bolded italicized** items are Bushcraft suggested.

Trip to _____ # Days _____

Trip Type ☐ Camp ☐ Glamp ☐ Bushcraft Dates _____

Tent/Shelter	#	LD
Tent/Hammock		
Rainfly		
Tent carpet		
Groundsheet/Tarp		
Guy Lines/Stakes		
Mallet/Hammer		
Tent Repair Kit		
Broom/Dustpan		
Sleeping system		
Sleeping Bag		
Sleeping Pad		
Blanket		
Pillow		
Inside/Outside Rug		
Sleeping Cot		
Tent Fan/Heater		
Camp Equipment		
Shelter/Canopy		
Chair		
Table		
Gear		
Backpack/Bag		
Gear Bag		
Knife/Multi-Tool		
Shovel		
Rope		
Strap/Bungee Cords		
Compass		
First Aid Kit		
Saw/Hatchet/Ax		
Duct Tape		
Work Gloves		
Activities		
Hiking/Biking Gear		

Kitchen/Cooking	#	LD
Canopy/Tarp		
Camp Kitchen		
Portable Grill/Grate		
Gas/Electric Stove & Fuel		
Dutch Oven & DO Lifter		
Pots / Pans / Skillet		
Cooler		
Table		
Water Jug		
Trash Can & Bags		
Drink/Coffee Cups		
Charcoal & Starter		
Dish/Biodegradable Soap		
Clothe & Paper Towels		
Grill Utensils/Oven Mitt		
Pots/Dishes		
Mess Kit		
Aluminum Foil		
Big Cutting Knives		
Frying Pan/Spatula		
Coffee Pot/Press/Maker		
Bottle/Wine Opener		
Wipes		
Ice		
Campfire		
Local Firewood		
Matches/Lighter/Starter		
Fire Extinguisher		
Roasting Sticks		
Electrical		
Flashlight		
Headlamp/Floodlight		
Lantern Fuel/Electric		
Extension Cord		
Extra Batteries / Charger		
Activities		
Fishing Gear / Bait		

Personal	#	LD
GUYS		
Jacket/Coat		
Shirts		
Pants		
Shorts		
Underwear		
Hygiene Kit		
Hat / Visor		
Socks		
Shoes / Boots		
Rain Gear		
Swimwear		
Sleepwear		
GIRLS		
Jacket/Coat		
Shirts/Blouses		
Pants		
Shorts		
Underwear		
Hygiene Kit		
Hat/Visor		
Socks		
Shoes/Boots		
Rain Gear		
Swimwear		
Sleepwear		
Misc		
Sunscreen/Bug Spray		
Bath Cloth/Towels		
Sunglasses		
Bandana		
Binoculars		
Activities		
Board Games/Cards		

PERSONAL ITEMS / FIRST AID

This checklist is for packing personal items for hygiene, miscellaneous, and first aid. The personal item section is designed for 4 people. To add more adults or children, just make a line to the right of the item. Use blank spaces for additional items.

Personal Item	Camper #1 ✓ | #	Camper #2 ✓ | #	Camper #3 ✓ | #	Camper #4 ✓ | #
Soap				
Toothbrush				
Toothpaste				
Dental Floss				
Deodorant				
Shampoo/Conditioner				
Comb/Brush				
Tissues				
Razor				
Shaving Cream				
Hand Sanitizer				
Cotton Tips				
Lotion				
Mouthwash				
Dental Floss				
Chapstick/Lip Balm				
Toilet Paper				
Tweezers				
Sunscreen				
Insect Repellent				
Washcloth				
Towel				
Mirror				
Hair Dryer				
Contacts/Case				
Saline Solution				
Nail Clippers/File				
Ear Plugs				
Medications				

First Aid Kit Checklist

First Aid Item	✓ | #
Band Aids	
Gauze Pads	
Antiseptic Wipes	
Hydrogen Peroxide	
Cotton Balls	
Sanitizer	
Tweezers	
Scissors	
Instant Cold/Hot Packs	
Latex Gloves	
Blanket	
Oral Thermometer	
Adhesive Tape	
Antibiotic Ointment	
Antihistamines	
Crepe Bandages	
Hydrocortisone	
Painkillers	
Safety Pins	
CPR Mouthpiece	
Alcohol Wipes	
Aspirin	
Calamine Lotion	
Splint	
Sterile Eye Dressings	
Medications	
Bandana/Wraps	
First Aid Manual	

4-DAY CAMPING MEAL PLANNER

Great meals make great camping! However, preparing and cooking meals outdoors requires accurate planning to have the right ingredients and equipment for culinary success. Here is a basic meal planning guide for each meal, ingredients, cooking equipment / methods, and grocery list items. Write "Travel" for meals not needed. Use 2 Sheets For 5+Days.

MEALS	TYPE OF MEAL/FOOD	COOKING METHOD	GROCERY ITEMS/LIST	✓
Example	Sandwiches / Chips / Fruits	SK/None	Bread, Cold Cuts, Chips, Fruits	✓
DAY 1 Breakfast				
Snack				
Lunch				
Snack				
Dinner				
Treat				
DAY 2 Breakfast				
Snack				
Lunch				
Snack				
Dinner				
Treat				
DAY 3 Breakfast				
Snack				
Lunch				
Snack				
Dinner				
Treat				
DAY 4 Breakfast				
Snack				
Lunch				
Snack				
Dinner				
Treat				

*Cooking Methods: **(S)** Stove **(G)** Grill **(F)** Firepit **(D)** Dutch Oven **(H)** Hanging Pot **(Sk)** Skillet

Drinks ☐ Milk ☐ Soda ☐ Tea ☐ Coffee ☐ Drink Mix

Spices	**Condiments**	**Fruit**	**Nuts/Mix**	**Fixings**
☐ Salt	☐ Ketchup	☐ Apples	☐ Nuts/Seeds	☐ Lettuce
☐ Pepper	☐ Mustard	☐ Bananas	☐ Trail Mix	☐ Tomatoes
☐ Sugar	☐ Relish	☐ Oranges	☐ Power Bars	☐ Pickes
☐ Hot Sauce	☐ Salsa	☐ Grapefruit	☐ Fruit Bars	☐ Onions
☐ _____	☐ _____	☐ _____	☐ _____	☐ _____

POST-TRIP REVIEW

To make every camping trip better, it's important to capture and review what you liked and what you would change. Use this sheet to review and plan your next adventure.

Campground Name _____ Dates _____ To _____

Address Street _____ City _____ State _____

Type of Site/Park ☐ National ☐ State ☐ Private Campsite # _____

Types of Campsite ☐ Managed/RV ☐ Primitive ☐ Boondocking ☐ Wilderness

Types of Trip ☐ Basic Camping ☐ Glamping (Tent/Rental/RV)
☐ Bushcraft ☐ Primitive ☐ Combination

Sites/Excursions Along the Way

1 _____ 2 _____ 3 _____

Designated Tent / Pad Sites? ☐ Yes ☐ No Campsite # _____

Campground Amenities

☐ Drinking Water (close/far)   ☐ Picnic   ☐ Firewood For Sale
☐ Fire Pits/Ring   ☐ Table – RV (120V 50A/30A)   ☐ Pet Friendly
☐ Tent Pads   ☐ Hookups   ☐ Nice Town
☐ BBQ Grill   ☐ Campground Store

What You Liked / What Went Well?

1 _____

2 _____

Other _____ Restrooms: Yes / No – Close / Far – Clean / Unclean – Shower / Electricity

What You Didn't Like / What Would You Change?

1 _____

2 _____

Animal Sightings _____

Biggest Surprise OR Need That The Campground Had (Or Didn't Have)?_____

Types of Activities Did You Do? (In Tent, Campsite, Campground, Local Areas, etc.)

_____

Things (activities / side trips) To Do Next Time?

_____

People You Met?

Name _____ From City/State _____ Phone/Email _____

Name _____ From City/State _____ Phone/Email _____

Name _____ From City/State _____ Phone/Email _____

TRIP EXPERIENCES

PICTURES · MEMORIES · MAPS · MISC. · NOTES

Notes

_____

_____

_____

_____

CAMPING TRIP PLANNING

Ready for your next great outdoor adventure? Use this worksheet to plan your trip and have the greatest "under the stars" experience possible.

What type of trip?

☐ Camping
☐ Tent Glamping
☐ Bushcraft
☐ Backpacking
☐ Combination

Why are you going?

☐ Fun
☐ Activities
☐ Alone Time
☐ Relaxation
☐ Develop and Test New Skills
☐ Others
_____

When will you go on your trip? Dates _____ to _____

Season _____ Seasonal Concerns _____

Location

City _____ ST _____ Park Name _____

Reservations Required? ☐ Yes ☐ No   ☐ Phone ☐ Web

Reservation # _____

Who is going? Name(s)

_____   _____
_____   _____

New Camping Skills and Preparation (Pitching Tent, Shelter Building, Fire Starting, Cooking, Hunting, Scavenging, Trapping, etc.) **Preparation** (Read, videos, testing, training, certification, etc.)

- Skill _____ How will you prep/test? _____
- Skill _____ How will you prep/test? _____

Special Gear/Equipment (New Type of Tent, Gas Equipment, Generator, Backpacks, Hunting, etc.)

1 _____   2 _____   3 _____

Gear to be purchased, rented or repaired?

1. Type of Gear _____ Purchase, rented, repaired? _____
2. Type of Gear _____ Purchase, rented, repaired? _____

How are you prepared for rain, cold, heat, wind, bugs and varmints?

Rain _____   Cold/Heat _____
Bugs _____   Varmints/Bears _____

Major Activities – What are the different activities you will do?

	Activity	Location
Day 1	_____	_____
Day 2	_____	_____
Day 3	_____	_____
Day 4	_____	_____

Nearest Emergency Room or Help

Facility_____ Address _____ Phone _____ Hours _____

Who Knows You're Gone Name _____ Phone _____ Email _____

GEAR AND EQUIPMENT CHECKLIST

This is a basic checklist for camping, glamping & bushcraft trips. There are categories and specific camping items. Put an "X" or number in the "#" column in red or blue ink. If you don't want to take an item, then strike through it (e.g. ~~Hammock~~). Once you've loaded an item, mark an X in the LD (Loaded) column. Blanks are for add-ons. **Bolded italicized** items are Bushcraft suggested.

Trip to _____ # Days _____

Trip Type ☐ Camp   ☐ Glamp   ☐ Bushcraft   Dates _____

Tent/Shelter	#	LD
Tent/Hammock		
Rainfly		
Tent carpet		
Groundsheet/Tarp		
Guy Lines/Stakes		
Mallet/Hammer		
Tent Repair Kit		
Broom/Dustpan		
Sleeping system		
Sleeping Bag		
Sleeping Pad		
Blanket		
Pillow		
Inside/Outside Rug		
Sleeping Cot		
Tent Fan/Heater		
Camp Equipment		
Shelter/Canopy		
Chair		
Table		
Gear		
Backpack/Bag		
Gear Bag		
Knife/Multi-Tool		
Shovel		
Rope		
Strap/Bungee Cords		
Compass		
First Aid Kit		
Saw/Hatchet/Ax		
Duct Tape		
Work Gloves		
Activities		
Hiking/Biking Gear		

Kitchen/Cooking	#	LD
Canopy/Tarp		
Camp Kitchen		
Portable Grill/Grate		
Gas/Electric Stove & Fuel		
Dutch Oven & DO Lifter		
Pots / Pans / Skillet		
Cooler		
Table		
Water Jug		
Trash Can & Bags		
Drink/Coffee Cups		
Charcoal & Starter		
Dish/Biodegradable Soap		
Clothe & Paper Towels		
Grill Utensils/Oven Mitt		
Pots/Dishes		
Mess Kit		
Aluminum Foil		
Big Cutting Knives		
Frying Pan/Spatula		
Coffee Pot/Press/Maker		
Bottle/Wine Opener		
Wipes		
Ice		
Campfire		
Local Firewood		
Matches/Lighter/Starter		
Fire Extinguisher		
Roasting Sticks		
Electrical		
Flashlight		
Headlamp/Floodlight		
Lantern Fuel/Electric		
Extension Cord		
Extra Batteries / Charger		
Activities		
Fishing Gear / Bait		

Personal	#	LD
GUYS		
Jacket/Coat		
Shirts		
Pants		
Shorts		
Underwear		
Hygiene Kit		
Hat / Visor		
Socks		
Shoes / Boots		
Rain Gear		
Swimwear		
Sleepwear		
GIRLS		
Jacket/Coat		
Shirts/Blouses		
Pants		
Shorts		
Underwear		
Hygiene Kit		
Hat/Visor		
Socks		
Shoes/Boots		
Rain Gear		
Swimwear		
Sleepwear		
Misc		
Sunscreen/Bug Spray		
Bath Cloth/Towels		
Sunglasses		
Bandana		
Binoculars		
Activities		
Board Games/Cards		

PERSONAL ITEMS / FIRST AID

This checklist is for packing personal items for hygiene, miscellaneous, and first aid. The personal item section is designed for 4 people. To add more adults or children, just make a line to the right of the item. Use blank spaces for additional items.

Personal Item	Camper #1 ✓ | #	Camper #2 ✓ | #	Camper #3 ✓ | #	Camper #4 ✓ | #
Soap				
Toothbrush				
Toothpaste				
Dental Floss				
Deodorant				
Shampoo/Conditioner				
Comb/Brush				
Tissues				
Razor				
Shaving Cream				
Hand Sanitizer				
Cotton Tips				
Lotion				
Mouthwash				
Dental Floss				
Chapstick/Lip Balm				
Toilet Paper				
Tweezers				
Sunscreen				
Insect Repellent				
Washcloth				
Towel				
Mirror				
Hair Dryer				
Contacts/Case				
Saline Solution				
Nail Clippers/File				
Ear Plugs				
Medications				

First Aid Kit Checklist

First Aid Item	✓ | #
Band Aids	
Gauze Pads	
Antiseptic Wipes	
Hydrogen Peroxide	
Cotton Balls	
Sanitizer	
Tweezers	
Scissors	
Instant Cold/Hot Packs	
Latex Gloves	
Blanket	
Oral Thermometer	
Adhesive Tape	
Antibiotic Ointment	
Antihistamines	
Crepe Bandages	
Hydrocortisone	
Painkillers	
Safety Pins	
CPR Mouthpiece	
Alcohol Wipes	
Aspirin	
Calamine Lotion	
Splint	
Sterile Eye Dressings	
Medications	
Bandana/Wraps	
First Aid Manual	

4-DAY CAMPING MEAL PLANNER

Great meals make great camping! However, preparing and cooking meals outdoors requires accurate planning to have the right ingredients and equipment for culinary success. Here is a basic meal planning guide for each meal, ingredients, cooking equipment / methods, and grocery list items. Write "Travel" for meals not needed. Use 2 Sheets For 5+Days.

	MEALS	TYPE OF MEAL/FOOD	COOKING METHOD	GROCERY ITEMS/LIST	✓
	Example	Sandwiches / Chips / Fruits	SK/None	Bread, Cold Cuts, Chips, Fruits	✓
DAY 1	Breakfast				
	Snack				
	Lunch				
	Snack				
	Dinner				
	Treat				
DAY 2	Breakfast				
	Snack				
	Lunch				
	Snack				
	Dinner				
	Treat				
DAY 3	Breakfast				
	Snack				
	Lunch				
	Snack				
	Dinner				
	Treat				
DAY 4	Breakfast				
	Snack				
	Lunch				
	Snack				
	Dinner				
	Treat				

*Cooking Methods: (S) Stove (G) Grill (F) Firepit (D) Dutch Oven (H) Hanging Pot (Sk) Skillet

Drinks ☐ Milk ☐ Soda ☐ Tea ☐ Coffee ☐ Drink Mix

Spices	**Condiments**	**Fruit**	**Nuts/Mix**	**Fixings**
☐ Salt	☐ Ketchup	☐ Apples	☐ Nuts/Seeds	☐ Lettuce
☐ Pepper	☐ Mustard	☐ Bananas	☐ Trail Mix	☐ Tomatoes
☐ Sugar	☐ Relish	☐ Oranges	☐ Power Bars	☐ Pickes
☐ Hot Sauce	☐ Salsa	☐ Grapefruit	☐ Fruit Bars	☐ Onions
☐ _____	☐ _____	☐ _____	☐ _____	☐ _____

POST-TRIP REVIEW

To make every camping trip better, it's important to capture and review what you liked and what you would change. Use this sheet to review and plan your next adventure.

Campground Name _____ Dates _____ To _____

Address Street _____ City _____ State _____

Type of Site/Park ☐ National ☐ State ☐ Private Campsite # _____

Types of Campsite ☐ Managed/RV ☐ Primitive ☐ Boondocking ☐ Wilderness

Types of Trip ☐ Basic Camping ☐ Glamping (Tent/Rental/RV)
☐ Bushcraft ☐ Primitive ☐ Combination

Sites/Excursions Along the Way

1 _____ 2 _____ 3 _____

Designated Tent / Pad Sites? ☐ Yes ☐ No Campsite # _____

Campground Amenities

☐ Drinking Water (close/far)   ☐ Picnic   ☐ Firewood For Sale
☐ Fire Pits/Ring   ☐ Table – RV (120V 50A/30A)   ☐ Pet Friendly
☐ Tent Pads   ☐ Hookups   ☐ Nice Town
☐ BBQ Grill   ☐ Campground Store

What You Liked / What Went Well?

1 _____

2 _____

Other _____ Restrooms: Yes / No – Close / Far – Clean / Unclean – Shower / Electricity

What You Didn't Like / What Would You Change?

1 _____

2 _____

Animal Sightings _____

Biggest Surprise OR Need That The Campground Had (Or Didn't Have)?_____

Types of Activities Did You Do? (In Tent, Campsite, Campground, Local Areas, etc.)

_____

Things (activities / side trips) To Do Next Time?

_____

People You Met?

Name _____ From City/State _____ Phone/Email _____
Name _____ From City/State _____ Phone/Email _____
Name _____ From City/State _____ Phone/Email _____

Notes

_____

_____

_____

_____

_____

CAMPING TRIP PLANNING

Ready for your next great outdoor adventure? Use this worksheet to plan your trip and have the greatest "under the stars" experience possible.

What type of trip?

☐ Camping
☐ Tent Glamping
☐ Bushcraft
☐ Backpacking
☐ Combination

Why are you going?

☐ Fun
☐ Activities
☐ Alone Time
☐ Relaxation
☐ Develop and Test New Skills
☐ Others
_____

When will you go on your trip? Dates _____ to _____

Season _____ Seasonal Concerns _____

Location

City _____ ST _____ Park Name _____

Reservations Required? ☐ Yes ☐ No   ☐ Phone ☐ Web

Reservation # _____

Who is going? Name(s)

_____   _____
_____   _____

New Camping Skills and Preparation (Pitching Tent, Shelter Building, Fire Starting, Cooking, Hunting, Scavenging, Trapping, etc.) **Preparation** (Read, videos, testing, training, certification, etc.)

• Skill _____ How will you prep/test? _____
• Skill _____ How will you prep/test? _____

Special Gear/Equipment (New Type of Tent, Gas Equipment, Generator, Backpacks, Hunting, etc.)

1 _____   2 _____   3 _____

Gear to be purchased, rented or repaired?

1. Type of Gear _____ Purchase, rented, repaired? _____
2. Type of Gear _____ Purchase, rented, repaired? _____

How are you prepared for rain, cold, heat, wind, bugs and varmints?

Rain _____   Cold/Heat _____
Bugs _____   Varmints/Bears _____

Major Activities – What are the different activities you will do?

	Activity	Location
Day 1	_____	_____
Day 2	_____	_____
Day 3	_____	_____
Day 4	_____	_____

Nearest Emergency Room or Help

Facility_____ Address _____ Phone _____ Hours _____

Who Knows You're Gone Name _____ Phone _____ Email _____

GEAR AND EQUIPMENT CHECKLIST

This is a basic checklist for camping, glamping & bushcraft trips. There are categories and specific camping items. Put an "X" or number in the "#" column in red or blue ink. If you don't want to take an item, then strike through it (e.g. ~~Hammock~~). Once you've loaded an item, mark an X in the LD (Loaded) column. Blanks are for add-ons. **Bolded italicized** items are Bushcraft suggested.

Trip to _____ # Days _____

Trip Type ☐ Camp ☐ Glamp ☐ Bushcraft Dates _____

Tent/Shelter	#	LD	Kitchen/Cooking	#	LD	Personal	#	LD
Tent/Hammock			Canopy/Tarp			**GUYS**		
Rainfly			Camp Kitchen			*Jacket/Coat*		
Tent carpet			Portable Grill/Grate			*Shirts*		
Groundsheet/Tarp			*Gas/Electric Stove & Fuel*			*Pants*		
Guy Lines/Stakes			Dutch Oven & DO Lifter			*Shorts*		
Mallet/Hammer			*Pots / Pans / Skillet*			*Underwear*		
Tent Repair Kit			Cooler			*Hygiene Kit*		
Broom/Dustpan			Table			*Hat / Visor*		
			Water Jug			*Socks*		
			Trash Can & Bags			*Shoes / Boots*		
Sleeping system			Drink/Coffee Cups			*Rain Gear*		
Sleeping Bag			Charcoal & Starter			Swimwear		
Sleeping Pad			Dish/Biodegradable Soap			Sleepwear		
Blanket			Clothe & Paper Towels					
Pillow			Grill Utensils/Oven Mitt					
Inside/Outside Rug			Pots/Dishes			**GIRLS**		
Sleeping Cot			*Mess Kit*			*Jacket/Coat*		
Tent Fan/Heater			Aluminum Foil			*Shirts/Blouses*		
			Big Cutting Knives			*Pants*		
			Frying Pan/Spatula			*Shorts*		
Camp Equipment			Coffee Pot/Press/Maker			*Underwear*		
Shelter/Canopy			Bottle/Wine Opener			*Hygiene Kit*		
Chair			Wipes			*Hat/Visor*		
Table			Ice			*Socks*		
						Shoes/Boots		
Gear			**Campfire**			*Rain Gear*		
Backpack/Bag			Local Firewood			Swimwear		
Gear Bag			*Matches/Lighter/Starter*			Sleepwear		
Knife/Multi-Tool			Fire Extinguisher					
Shovel			Roasting Sticks					
Rope						**Misc**		
Strap/Bungee Cords			**Electrical**			Sunscreen/Bug Spray		
Compass			Flashlight			Bath Cloth/Towels		
First Aid Kit			*Headlamp/Floodlight*			Sunglasses		
Saw/Hatchet/Ax			Lantern Fuel/Electric			*Bandana*		
Duct Tape			*Extension Cord*			Binoculars		
Work Gloves			Extra Batteries / Charger					
Activities			**Activities**			**Activities**		
Hiking/Biking Gear			*Fishing Gear / Bait*			Board Games/Cards		

PERSONAL ITEMS / FIRST AID

This checklist is for packing personal items for hygiene, miscellaneous, and first aid. The personal item section is designed for 4 people. To add more adults or children, just make a line to the right of the item. Use blank spaces for additional items.

Personal Item	Camper #1 ✓ | #	Camper #2 ✓ | #	Camper #3 ✓ | #	Camper #4 ✓ | #
Soap				
Toothbrush				
Toothpaste				
Dental Floss				
Deodorant				
Shampoo/Conditioner				
Comb/Brush				
Tissues				
Razor				
Shaving Cream				
Hand Sanitizer				
Cotton Tips				
Lotion				
Mouthwash				
Dental Floss				
Chapstick/Lip Balm				
Toilet Paper				
Tweezers				
Sunscreen				
Insect Repellent				
Washcloth				
Towel				
Mirror				
Hair Dryer				
Contacts/Case				
Saline Solution				
Nail Clippers/File				
Ear Plugs				
Medications				

First Aid Kit Checklist

First Aid Item	✓ | #
Band Aids	
Gauze Pads	
Antiseptic Wipes	
Hydrogen Peroxide	
Cotton Balls	
Sanitizer	
Tweezers	
Scissors	
Instant Cold/Hot Packs	
Latex Gloves	
Blanket	
Oral Thermometer	
Adhesive Tape	
Antibiotic Ointment	
Antihistamines	
Crepe Bandages	
Hydrocortisone	
Painkillers	
Safety Pins	
CPR Mouthpiece	
Alcohol Wipes	
Aspirin	
Calamine Lotion	
Splint	
Sterile Eye Dressings	
Medications	
Bandana/Wraps	
First Aid Manual	

4-DAY CAMPING MEAL PLANNER

Great meals make great camping! However, preparing and cooking meals outdoors requires accurate planning to have the right ingredients and equipment for culinary success. Here is a basic meal planning guide for each meal, ingredients, cooking equipment / methods, and grocery list items. Write "Travel" for meals not needed. Use 2 Sheets For 5+Days.

	MEALS	TYPE OF MEAL/FOOD	COOKING METHOD	GROCERY ITEMS/LIST	✓
	Example	Sandwiches / Chips / Fruits	SK/None	Bread, Cold Cuts, Chips, Fruits	✓
DAY 1	Breakfast				
	Snack				
	Lunch				
	Snack				
	Dinner				
	Treat				
DAY 2	Breakfast				
	Snack				
	Lunch				
	Snack				
	Dinner				
	Treat				
DAY 3	Breakfast				
	Snack				
	Lunch				
	Snack				
	Dinner				
	Treat				
DAY 4	Breakfast				
	Snack				
	Lunch				
	Snack				
	Dinner				
	Treat				

*Cooking Methods: **(S)** Stove   **(G)** Grill   **(F)** Firepit   **(D)** Dutch Oven   **(H)** Hanging Pot   **(Sk)** Skillet

Drinks   ☐ Milk   ☐ Soda   ☐ Tea   ☐ Coffee   ☐ Drink Mix

Spices	**Condiments**	**Fruit**	**Nuts/Mix**	**Fixings**
☐ Salt	☐ Ketchup	☐ Apples	☐ Nuts/Seeds	☐ Lettuce
☐ Pepper	☐ Mustard	☐ Bananas	☐ Trail Mix	☐ Tomatoes
☐ Sugar	☐ Relish	☐ Oranges	☐ Power Bars	☐ Pickes
☐ Hot Sauce	☐ Salsa	☐ Grapefruit	☐ Fruit Bars	☐ Onions
☐ _____	☐ _____	☐ _____	☐ _____	☐ _____

POST-TRIP REVIEW

To make every camping trip better, it's important to capture and review what you liked and what you would change. Use this sheet to review and plan your next adventure.

Campground Name _____ Dates _____ To _____

Address Street _____ City _____ State _____

Type of Site/Park ☐ National ☐ State ☐ Private Campsite # _____

Types of Campsite ☐ Managed/RV ☐ Primitive ☐ Boondocking ☐ Wilderness

Types of Trip ☐ Basic Camping ☐ Glamping (Tent/Rental/RV)
☐ Bushcraft ☐ Primitive ☐ Combination

Sites/Excursions Along the Way

1 _____ 2 _____ 3 _____

Designated Tent / Pad Sites? ☐ Yes ☐ No Campsite # _____

Campground Amenities

☐ Drinking Water (close/far)   ☐ Picnic   ☐ Firewood For Sale
☐ Fire Pits/Ring   ☐ Table – RV (120V 50A/30A)   ☐ Pet Friendly
☐ Tent Pads   ☐ Hookups   ☐ Nice Town
☐ BBQ Grill   ☐ Campground Store

What You Liked / What Went Well?

1 _____
2 _____

Other _____ Restrooms: Yes / No – Close / Far – Clean / Unclean – Shower / Electricity

What You Didn't Like / What Would You Change?

1 _____
2 _____

Animal Sightings _____

Biggest Surprise OR Need That The Campground Had (Or Didn't Have)? _____

Types of Activities Did You Do? (In Tent, Campsite, Campground, Local Areas, etc.)

_____

Things (activities / side trips) To Do Next Time?

_____

People You Met?

Name _____ From City/State _____ Phone/Email _____
Name _____ From City/State _____ Phone/Email _____
Name _____ From City/State _____ Phone/Email _____

TRIP EXPERIENCES

Notes

_____

_____

_____

_____

_____

CAMPING TRIP PLANNING

Ready for your next great outdoor adventure? Use this worksheet to plan your trip and have the greatest "under the stars" experience possible.

What type of trip?

☐ Camping
☐ Tent Glamping
☐ Bushcraft
☐ Backpacking
☐ Combination

Why are you going?

☐ Fun
☐ Activities
☐ Alone Time
☐ Relaxation
☐ Develop and Test New Skills
☐ Others
_____

When will you go on your trip? Dates _____ to _____

Season _____ Seasonal Concerns _____

Location

City _____ ST _____ Park Name _____

Reservations Required? ☐ Yes ☐ No ☐ Phone ☐ Web

Reservation # _____

Who is going? Name(s)

_____ _____

_____ _____

New Camping Skills and Preparation (Pitching Tent, Shelter Building, Fire Starting, Cooking, Hunting, Scavenging, Trapping, etc.) **Preparation** (Read, videos, testing, training, certification, etc.)

• Skill _____ How will you prep/test? _____
• Skill _____ How will you prep/test? _____

Special Gear/Equipment (New Type of Tent, Gas Equipment, Generator, Backpacks, Hunting, etc.)

1 _____ 2 _____ 3 _____

Gear to be purchased, rented or repaired?

1. Type of Gear _____ Purchase, rented, repaired? _____
2. Type of Gear _____ Purchase, rented, repaired? _____

How are you prepared for rain, cold, heat, wind, bugs and varmints?

Rain _____ Cold/Heat _____
Bugs _____ Varmints/Bears _____

Major Activities – What are the different activities you will do?

	Activity	Location
Day 1	_____	_____
Day 2	_____	_____
Day 3	_____	_____
Day 4	_____	_____

Nearest Emergency Room or Help

Facility_____ Address _____ Phone _____ Hours _____

Who Knows You're Gone Name _____ Phone _____ Email _____

GEAR AND EQUIPMENT CHECKLIST

This is a basic checklist for camping, glamping & bushcraft trips. There are categories and specific camping items. Put an "X" or number in the "#" column in red or blue ink. If you don't want to take an item, then strike through it (e.g. ~~Hammock~~). Once you've loaded an item, mark an X in the LD (Loaded) column. Blanks are for add-ons. **Bolded italicized** items are Bushcraft suggested.

Trip to _____ # Days _____

Trip Type ☐ Camp ☐ Glamp ☐ Bushcraft Dates _____

Tent/Shelter	#	LD	Kitchen/Cooking	#	LD	Personal	#	LD
Tent/Hammock			Canopy/Tarp			**GUYS**		
Rainfly			Camp Kitchen			*Jacket/Coat*		
Tent carpet			Portable Grill/Grate			*Shirts*		
Groundsheet/Tarp			Gas/Electric Stove & Fuel			*Pants*		
Guy Lines/Stakes			Dutch Oven & DO Lifter			*Shorts*		
Mallet/Hammer			*Pots / Pans / Skillet*			*Underwear*		
Tent Repair Kit			Cooler			*Hygiene Kit*		
Broom/Dustpan			Table			*Hat / Visor*		
			Water Jug			*Socks*		
Sleeping system			Trash Can & Bags			*Shoes / Boots*		
Sleeping Bag			Drink/Coffee Cups			*Rain Gear*		
Sleeping Pad			Charcoal & Starter			Swimwear		
Blanket			Dish/Biodegradable Soap			Sleepwear		
Pillow			Clothe & Paper Towels					
Inside/Outside Rug			Grill Utensils/Oven Mitt					
Sleeping Cot			Pots/Dishes			**GIRLS**		
Tent Fan/Heater			*Mess Kit*			*Jacket/Coat*		
			Aluminum Foil			*Shirts/Blouses*		
			Big Cutting Knives			*Pants*		
Camp Equipment			Frying Pan/Spatula			*Shorts*		
Shelter/Canopy			Coffee Pot/Press/Maker			*Underwear*		
Chair			Bottle/Wine Opener			*Hygiene Kit*		
Table			Wipes			*Hat/Visor*		
			Ice			*Socks*		
Gear						*Shoes/Boots*		
Backpack/Bag			**Campfire**			*Rain Gear*		
Gear Bag			Local Firewood			Swimwear		
Knife/Multi-Tool			*Matches/Lighter/Starter*			Sleepwear		
Shovel			Fire Extinguisher					
Rope			Roasting Sticks					
Strap/Bungee Cords								
Compass			**Electrical**			**Misc**		
First Aid Kit			Flashlight			Sunscreen/Bug Spray		
Saw/Hatchet/Ax			*Headlamp/Floodlight*			Bath Cloth/Towels		
Duct Tape			Lantern Fuel/Electric			Sunglasses		
Work Gloves			*Extension Cord*			*Bandana*		
			Extra Batteries / Charger			Binoculars		
Activities			**Activities**			**Activities**		
Hiking/Biking Gear			*Fishing Gear / Bait*			Board Games/Cards		

PERSONAL ITEMS / FIRST AID

This checklist is for packing personal items for hygiene, miscellaneous, and first aid. The personal item section is designed for 4 people. To add more adults or children, just make a line to the right of the item. Use blank spaces for additional items.

Personal Item	Camper #1 ✓ | #	Camper #2 ✓ | #	Camper #3 ✓ | #	Camper #4 ✓ | #
Soap				
Toothbrush				
Toothpaste				
Dental Floss				
Deodorant				
Shampoo/Conditioner				
Comb/Brush				
Tissues				
Razor				
Shaving Cream				
Hand Sanitizer				
Cotton Tips				
Lotion				
Mouthwash				
Dental Floss				
Chapstick/Lip Balm				
Toilet Paper				
Tweezers				
Sunscreen				
Insect Repellent				
Washcloth				
Towel				
Mirror				
Hair Dryer				
Contacts/Case				
Saline Solution				
Nail Clippers/File				
Ear Plugs				
Medications				

First Aid Kit Checklist

First Aid Item	✓ | #
Band Aids	
Gauze Pads	
Antiseptic Wipes	
Hydrogen Peroxide	
Cotton Balls	
Sanitizer	
Tweezers	
Scissors	
Instant Cold/Hot Packs	
Latex Gloves	
Blanket	
Oral Thermometer	
Adhesive Tape	
Antibiotic Ointment	
Antihistamines	
Crepe Bandages	
Hydrocortisone	
Painkillers	
Safety Pins	
CPR Mouthpiece	
Alcohol Wipes	
Aspirin	
Calamine Lotion	
Splint	
Sterile Eye Dressings	
Medications	
Bandana/Wraps	
First Aid Manual	

4-DAY CAMPING MEAL PLANNER

Great meals make great camping! However, preparing and cooking meals outdoors requires accurate planning to have the right ingredients and equipment for culinary success. Here is a basic meal planning guide for each meal, ingredients, cooking equipment / methods, and grocery list items. Write "Travel" for meals not needed. Use 2 Sheets For 5+Days.

	MEALS	TYPE OF MEAL/FOOD	COOKING METHOD	GROCERY ITEMS/LIST	✓
	Example	Sandwiches / Chips / Fruits	SK/None	Bread, Cold Cuts, Chips, Fruits	✓
DAY 1	Breakfast				
	Snack				
	Lunch				
	Snack				
	Dinner				
	Treat				
DAY 2	Breakfast				
	Snack				
	Lunch				
	Snack				
	Dinner				
	Treat				
DAY 3	Breakfast				
	Snack				
	Lunch				
	Snack				
	Dinner				
	Treat				
DAY 4	Breakfast				
	Snack				
	Lunch				
	Snack				
	Dinner				
	Treat				

*Cooking Methods: **(S)** Stove **(G)** Grill **(F)** Firepit **(D)** Dutch Oven **(H)** Hanging Pot **(Sk)** Skillet

Drinks ☐ Milk ☐ Soda ☐ Tea ☐ Coffee ☐ Drink Mix

Spices	**Condiments**	**Fruit**	**Nuts/Mix**	**Fixings**
☐ Salt	☐ Ketchup	☐ Apples	☐ Nuts/Seeds	☐ Lettuce
☐ Pepper	☐ Mustard	☐ Bananas	☐ Trail Mix	☐ Tomatoes
☐ Sugar	☐ Relish	☐ Oranges	☐ Power Bars	☐ Pickes
☐ Hot Sauce	☐ Salsa	☐ Grapefruit	☐ Fruit Bars	☐ Onions
☐ _____	☐ _____	☐ _____	☐ _____	☐ _____

POST-TRIP REVIEW

To make every camping trip better, it's important to capture and review what you liked and what you would change. Use this sheet to review and plan your next adventure.

Campground Name _____ Dates _____ To _____

Address Street _____ City _____ State _____

Type of Site/Park ☐ National   ☐ State   ☐ Private   Campsite # _____

Types of Campsite ☐ Managed/RV   ☐ Primitive   ☐ Boondocking   ☐ Wilderness

Types of Trip ☐ Basic Camping   ☐ Glamping (Tent/Rental/RV)
☐ Bushcraft   ☐ Primitive   ☐ Combination

Sites/Excursions Along the Way

1 _____   2 _____   3 _____

Designated Tent / Pad Sites?   ☐ Yes   ☐ No   Campsite # _____

Campground Amenities

☐ Drinking Water (close/far)   ☐ Picnic   ☐ Firewood For Sale
☐ Fire Pits/Ring   ☐ Table – RV (120V 50A/30A)   ☐ Pet Friendly
☐ Tent Pads   ☐ Hookups   ☐ Nice Town
☐ BBQ Grill   ☐ Campground Store

What You Liked / What Went Well?

1 _____
2 _____

Other _____ Restrooms: Yes / No – Close / Far – Clean / Unclean – Shower / Electricity

What You Didn't Like / What Would You Change?

1 _____
2 _____

Animal Sightings _____

Biggest Surprise OR Need That The Campground Had (Or Didn't Have)? _____

Types of Activities Did You Do? (In Tent, Campsite, Campground, Local Areas, etc.)

_____

Things (activities / side trips) To Do Next Time?

_____

People You Met?

Name _____ From City/State _____ Phone/Email _____
Name _____ From City/State _____ Phone/Email _____
Name _____ From City/State _____ Phone/Email _____

Notes

_____

_____

_____

_____

_____

CAMPING TRIP PLANNING

Ready for your next great outdoor adventure? Use this worksheet to plan your trip and have the greatest "under the stars" experience possible.

What type of trip?

☐ Camping
☐ Tent Glamping
☐ Bushcraft
☐ Backpacking
☐ Combination

Why are you going?

☐ Fun
☐ Activities
☐ Alone Time
☐ Relaxation
☐ Develop and Test New Skills
☐ Others
_____

When will you go on your trip? Dates _____ to _____

Season _____ Seasonal Concerns _____

Location

City _____ ST _____ Park Name _____

Reservations Required? ☐ Yes ☐ No   ☐ Phone ☐ Web

Reservation # _____

Who is going? Name(s)

_____   _____
_____   _____

New Camping Skills and Preparation (Pitching Tent, Shelter Building, Fire Starting, Cooking, Hunting, Scavenging, Trapping, etc.) **Preparation** (Read, videos, testing, training, certification, etc.)

- Skill _____ How will you prep/test? _____
- Skill _____ How will you prep/test? _____

Special Gear/Equipment (New Type of Tent, Gas Equipment, Generator, Backpacks, Hunting, etc.)

1 _____   2 _____   3 _____

Gear to be purchased, rented or repaired?

1. Type of Gear _____ Purchase, rented, repaired? _____
2. Type of Gear _____ Purchase, rented, repaired? _____

How are you prepared for rain, cold, heat, wind, bugs and varmints?

Rain _____   Cold/Heat _____
Bugs _____   Varmints/Bears _____

Major Activities – What are the different activities you will do?

	Activity	Location
Day 1	_____	_____
Day 2	_____	_____
Day 3	_____	_____
Day 4	_____	_____

Nearest Emergency Room or Help

Facility_____ Address _____ Phone _____ Hours _____

Who Knows You're Gone   Name _____ Phone _____ Email _____

GEAR AND EQUIPMENT CHECKLIST

This is a basic checklist for camping, glamping & bushcraft trips. There are categories and specific camping items. Put an "X" or number in the "#" column in red or blue ink. If you don't want to take an item, then strike through it (e.g. ~~Hammock~~). Once you've loaded an item, mark an X in the LD (Loaded) column. Blanks are for add-ons. **Bolded italicized** items are Bushcraft suggested.

Trip to _____ # Days _____

Trip Type ☐ Camp ☐ Glamp ☐ Bushcraft Dates _____

Tent/Shelter	#	LD
Tent/Hammock		
Rainfly		
Tent carpet		
Groundsheet/Tarp		
Guy Lines/Stakes		
Mallet/Hammer		
Tent Repair Kit		
Broom/Dustpan		
Sleeping system		
Sleeping Bag		
Sleeping Pad		
Blanket		
Pillow		
Inside/Outside Rug		
Sleeping Cot		
Tent Fan/Heater		
Camp Equipment		
Shelter/Canopy		
Chair		
Table		
Gear		
Backpack/Bag		
Gear Bag		
Knife/Multi-Tool		
Shovel		
Rope		
Strap/Bungee Cords		
Compass		
First Aid Kit		
Saw/Hatchet/Ax		
Duct Tape		
Work Gloves		
Activities		
Hiking/Biking Gear		

Kitchen/Cooking	#	LD
Canopy/Tarp		
Camp Kitchen		
Portable Grill/Grate		
Gas/Electric Stove & Fuel		
Dutch Oven & DO Lifter		
Pots / Pans / Skillet		
Cooler		
Table		
Water Jug		
Trash Can & Bags		
Drink/Coffee Cups		
Charcoal & Starter		
Dish/Biodegradable Soap		
Clothe & Paper Towels		
Grill Utensils/Oven Mitt		
Pots/Dishes		
Mess Kit		
Aluminum Foil		
Big Cutting Knives		
Frying Pan/Spatula		
Coffee Pot/Press/Maker		
Bottle/Wine Opener		
Wipes		
Ice		
Campfire		
Local Firewood		
Matches/Lighter/Starter		
Fire Extinguisher		
Roasting Sticks		
Electrical		
Flashlight		
Headlamp/Floodlight		
Lantern Fuel/Electric		
Extension Cord		
Extra Batteries / Charger		
Activities		
Fishing Gear / Bait		

Personal	#	LD
GUYS		
Jacket/Coat		
Shirts		
Pants		
Shorts		
Underwear		
Hygiene Kit		
Hat / Visor		
Socks		
Shoes / Boots		
Rain Gear		
Swimwear		
Sleepwear		
GIRLS		
Jacket/Coat		
Shirts/Blouses		
Pants		
Shorts		
Underwear		
Hygiene Kit		
Hat/Visor		
Socks		
Shoes/Boots		
Rain Gear		
Swimwear		
Sleepwear		
Misc		
Sunscreen/Bug Spray		
Bath Cloth/Towels		
Sunglasses		
Bandana		
Binoculars		
Activities		
Board Games/Cards		

PERSONAL ITEMS / FIRST AID

This checklist is for packing personal items for hygiene, miscellaneous, and first aid. The personal item section is designed for 4 people. To add more adults or children, just make a line to the right of the item. Use blank spaces for additional items.

Personal Item	Camper #1 ✓ | #	Camper #2 ✓ | #	Camper #3 ✓ | #	Camper #4 ✓ | #
Soap				
Toothbrush				
Toothpaste				
Dental Floss				
Deodorant				
Shampoo/Conditioner				
Comb/Brush				
Tissues				
Razor				
Shaving Cream				
Hand Sanitizer				
Cotton Tips				
Lotion				
Mouthwash				
Dental Floss				
Chapstick/Lip Balm				
Toilet Paper				
Tweezers				
Sunscreen				
Insect Repellent				
Washcloth				
Towel				
Mirror				
Hair Dryer				
Contacts/Case				
Saline Solution				
Nail Clippers/File				
Ear Plugs				
Medications				

First Aid Kit Checklist

First Aid Item	✓ | #
Band Aids	
Gauze Pads	
Antiseptic Wipes	
Hydrogen Peroxide	
Cotton Balls	
Sanitizer	
Tweezers	
Scissors	
Instant Cold/Hot Packs	
Latex Gloves	
Blanket	
Oral Thermometer	
Adhesive Tape	
Antibiotic Ointment	
Antihistamines	
Crepe Bandages	
Hydrocortisone	
Painkillers	
Safety Pins	
CPR Mouthpiece	
Alcohol Wipes	
Aspirin	
Calamine Lotion	
Splint	
Sterile Eye Dressings	
Medications	
Bandana/Wraps	
First Aid Manual	

4-DAY CAMPING MEAL PLANNER

Great meals make great camping! However, preparing and cooking meals outdoors requires accurate planning to have the right ingredients and equipment for culinary success. Here is a basic meal planning guide for each meal, ingredients, cooking equipment / methods, and grocery list items. Write "Travel" for meals not needed. Use 2 Sheets For 5+Days.

MEALS	TYPE OF MEAL/FOOD	COOKING METHOD	GROCERY ITEMS/LIST	✓
Example	Sandwiches / Chips / Fruits	SK/None	Bread, Cold Cuts, Chips, Fruits	✓
DAY 1 Breakfast				
Snack				
Lunch				
Snack				
Dinner				
Treat				
DAY 2 Breakfast				
Snack				
Lunch				
Snack				
Dinner				
Treat				
DAY 3 Breakfast				
Snack				
Lunch				
Snack				
Dinner				
Treat				
DAY 4 Breakfast				
Snack				
Lunch				
Snack				
Dinner				
Treat				

*Cooking Methods: **(S)** Stove   **(G)** Grill   **(F)** Firepit   **(D)** Dutch Oven   **(H)** Hanging Pot   **(Sk)** Skillet

Drinks   ☐ Milk   ☐ Soda   ☐ Tea   ☐ Coffee   ☐ Drink Mix

Spices	**Condiments**	**Fruit**	**Nuts/Mix**	**Fixings**
☐ Salt	☐ Ketchup	☐ Apples	☐ Nuts/Seeds	☐ Lettuce
☐ Pepper	☐ Mustard	☐ Bananas	☐ Trail Mix	☐ Tomatoes
☐ Sugar	☐ Relish	☐ Oranges	☐ Power Bars	☐ Pickes
☐ Hot Sauce	☐ Salsa	☐ Grapefruit	☐ Fruit Bars	☐ Onions
☐ _____	☐ _____	☐ _____	☐ _____	☐ _____

POST-TRIP REVIEW

To make every camping trip better, it's important to capture and review what you liked and what you would change. Use this sheet to review and plan your next adventure.

Campground Name _____ Dates _____ To _____

Address Street _____ City _____ State _____

Type of Site/Park ☐ National ☐ State ☐ Private Campsite # _____

Types of Campsite ☐ Managed/RV ☐ Primitive ☐ Boondocking ☐ Wilderness

Types of Trip ☐ Basic Camping ☐ Glamping (Tent/Rental/RV)
☐ Bushcraft ☐ Primitive ☐ Combination

Sites/Excursions Along the Way

1 _____ 2 _____ 3 _____

Designated Tent / Pad Sites? ☐ Yes ☐ No Campsite # _____

Campground Amenities

☐ Drinking Water (close/far)   ☐ Picnic   ☐ Firewood For Sale
☐ Fire Pits/Ring   ☐ Table – RV (120V 50A/30A)   ☐ Pet Friendly
☐ Tent Pads   ☐ Hookups   ☐ Nice Town
☐ BBQ Grill   ☐ Campground Store

What You Liked / What Went Well?

1 _____

2 _____

Other _____ Restrooms: Yes / No – Close / Far – Clean / Unclean – Shower / Electricity

What You Didn't Like / What Would You Change?

1 _____

2 _____

Animal Sightings _____

Biggest Surprise OR Need That The Campground Had (Or Didn't Have)? _____

Types of Activities Did You Do? (In Tent, Campsite, Campground, Local Areas, etc.)

_____

Things (activities / side trips) To Do Next Time?

_____

People You Met?

Name _____ From City/State _____ Phone/Email _____
Name _____ From City/State _____ Phone/Email _____
Name _____ From City/State _____ Phone/Email _____

TRIP EXPERIENCES

PICTURES · MEMORIES · MAPS · MISC. · NOTES

Notes

_____

_____

_____

_____

_____

CAMPING TRIP PLANNING

Ready for your next great outdoor adventure? Use this worksheet to plan your trip and have the greatest "under the stars" experience possible.

What type of trip?

☐ Camping
☐ Tent Glamping
☐ Bushcraft
☐ Backpacking
☐ Combination

Why are you going?

☐ Fun
☐ Activities
☐ Alone Time
☐ Relaxation
☐ Develop and
   Test New Skills
☐ Others
_____

When will you go on your trip? Dates _____ to _____

Season _____ Seasonal Concerns _____

Location

City _____ ST _____ Park Name _____

Reservations Required? ☐ Yes ☐ No   ☐ Phone ☐ Web

Reservation # _____

Who is going? Name(s)

_____ _____
_____ _____

New Camping Skills and Preparation (Pitching Tent, Shelter Building, Fire Starting, Cooking, Hunting, Scavenging, Trapping, etc.) **Preparation** (Read, videos, testing, training, certification, etc.)

• Skill _____ How will you prep/test? _____
• Skill _____ How will you prep/test? _____

Special Gear/Equipment (New Type of Tent, Gas Equipment, Generator, Backpacks, Hunting, etc.)

1 _____ 2 _____ 3 _____

Gear to be purchased, rented or repaired?

1. Type of Gear _____ Purchase, rented, repaired? _____
2. Type of Gear _____ Purchase, rented, repaired? _____

How are you prepared for rain, cold, heat, wind, bugs and varmints?

Rain _____ Cold/Heat _____
Bugs _____ Varmints/Bears _____

Major Activities – What are the different activities you will do?

	Activity	Location
Day 1	_____	_____
Day 2	_____	_____
Day 3	_____	_____
Day 4	_____	_____

Nearest Emergency Room or Help

Facility_____ Address _____ Phone _____ Hours _____

Who Knows You're Gone Name _____ Phone _____ Email _____

GEAR AND EQUIPMENT CHECKLIST

This is a basic checklist for camping, glamping & bushcraft trips. There are categories and specific camping items. Put an "X" or number in the "#" column in red or blue ink. If you don't want to take an item, then strike through it (e.g. ~~Hammock~~). Once you've loaded an item, mark an X in the LD (Loaded) column. Blanks are for add-ons. **Bolded italicized** items are Bushcraft suggested.

Trip to _____ # Days _____

Trip Type ☐ Camp   ☐ Glamp   ☐ Bushcraft   Dates _____

Tent/Shelter	#	LD
Tent/Hammock		
Rainfly		
Tent carpet		
Groundsheet/Tarp		
Guy Lines/Stakes		
Mallet/Hammer		
Tent Repair Kit		
Broom/Dustpan		
Sleeping system		
Sleeping Bag		
Sleeping Pad		
Blanket		
Pillow		
Inside/Outside Rug		
Sleeping Cot		
Tent Fan/Heater		
Camp Equipment		
Shelter/Canopy		
Chair		
Table		
Gear		
Backpack/Bag		
Gear Bag		
Knife/Multi-Tool		
Shovel		
Rope		
Strap/Bungee Cords		
Compass		
First Aid Kit		
Saw/Hatchet/Ax		
Duct Tape		
Work Gloves		
Activities		
Hiking/Biking Gear		

Kitchen/Cooking	#	LD
Canopy/Tarp		
Camp Kitchen		
Portable Grill/Grate		
Gas/Electric Stove & Fuel		
Dutch Oven & DO Lifter		
Pots / Pans / Skillet		
Cooler		
Table		
Water Jug		
Trash Can & Bags		
Drink/Coffee Cups		
Charcoal & Starter		
Dish/Biodegradable Soap		
Clothe & Paper Towels		
Grill Utensils/Oven Mitt		
Pots/Dishes		
Mess Kit		
Aluminum Foil		
Big Cutting Knives		
Frying Pan/Spatula		
Coffee Pot/Press/Maker		
Bottle/Wine Opener		
Wipes		
Ice		
Campfire		
Local Firewood		
Matches/Lighter/Starter		
Fire Extinguisher		
Roasting Sticks		
Electrical		
Flashlight		
Headlamp/Floodlight		
Lantern Fuel/Electric		
Extension Cord		
Extra Batteries / Charger		
Activities		
Fishing Gear / Bait		

Personal	#	LD
GUYS		
Jacket/Coat		
Shirts		
Pants		
Shorts		
Underwear		
Hygiene Kit		
Hat / Visor		
Socks		
Shoes / Boots		
Rain Gear		
Swimwear		
Sleepwear		
GIRLS		
Jacket/Coat		
Shirts/Blouses		
Pants		
Shorts		
Underwear		
Hygiene Kit		
Hat/Visor		
Socks		
Shoes/Boots		
Rain Gear		
Swimwear		
Sleepwear		
Misc		
Sunscreen/Bug Spray		
Bath Cloth/Towels		
Sunglasses		
Bandana		
Binoculars		
Activities		
Board Games/Cards		

PERSONAL ITEMS / FIRST AID

This checklist is for packing personal items for hygiene, miscellaneous, and first aid. The personal item section is designed for 4 people. To add more adults or children, just make a line to the right of the item. Use blank spaces for additional items.

Personal Item	Camper #1 ✓ | #	Camper #2 ✓ | #	Camper #3 ✓ | #	Camper #4 ✓ | #
Soap				
Toothbrush				
Toothpaste				
Dental Floss				
Deodorant				
Shampoo/Conditioner				
Comb/Brush				
Tissues				
Razor				
Shaving Cream				
Hand Sanitizer				
Cotton Tips				
Lotion				
Mouthwash				
Dental Floss				
Chapstick/Lip Balm				
Toilet Paper				
Tweezers				
Sunscreen				
Insect Repellent				
Washcloth				
Towel				
Mirror				
Hair Dryer				
Contacts/Case				
Saline Solution				
Nail Clippers/File				
Ear Plugs				
Medications				

First Aid Kit Checklist

First Aid Item	✓ | #
Band Aids	
Gauze Pads	
Antiseptic Wipes	
Hydrogen Peroxide	
Cotton Balls	
Sanitizer	
Tweezers	
Scissors	
Instant Cold/Hot Packs	
Latex Gloves	
Blanket	
Oral Thermometer	
Adhesive Tape	
Antibiotic Ointment	
Antihistamines	
Crepe Bandages	
Hydrocortisone	
Painkillers	
Safety Pins	
CPR Mouthpiece	
Alcohol Wipes	
Aspirin	
Calamine Lotion	
Splint	
Sterile Eye Dressings	
Medications	
Bandana/Wraps	
First Aid Manual	

4-DAY CAMPING MEAL PLANNER

Great meals make great camping! However, preparing and cooking meals outdoors requires accurate planning to have the right ingredients and equipment for culinary success. Here is a basic meal planning guide for each meal, ingredients, cooking equipment / methods, and grocery list items. Write "Travel" for meals not needed. Use 2 Sheets For 5+Days.

MEALS	TYPE OF MEAL/FOOD	COOKING METHOD	GROCERY ITEMS/LIST	✓
Example	Sandwiches / Chips / Fruits	SK/None	Bread, Cold Cuts, Chips, Fruits	✓
DAY 1 Breakfast				
Snack				
Lunch				
Snack				
Dinner				
Treat				
DAY 2 Breakfast				
Snack				
Lunch				
Snack				
Dinner				
Treat				
DAY 3 Breakfast				
Snack				
Lunch				
Snack				
Dinner				
Treat				
DAY 4 Breakfast				
Snack				
Lunch				
Snack				
Dinner				
Treat				

*Cooking Methods: **(S)** Stove   **(G)** Grill   **(F)** Firepit   **(D)** Dutch Oven   **(H)** Hanging Pot   **(Sk)** Skillet

Drinks   ☐ Milk   ☐ Soda   ☐ Tea   ☐ Coffee   ☐ Drink Mix

Spices	**Condiments**	**Fruit**	**Nuts/Mix**	**Fixings**
☐ Salt	☐ Ketchup	☐ Apples	☐ Nuts/Seeds	☐ Lettuce
☐ Pepper	☐ Mustard	☐ Bananas	☐ Trail Mix	☐ Tomatoes
☐ Sugar	☐ Relish	☐ Oranges	☐ Power Bars	☐ Pickes
☐ Hot Sauce	☐ Salsa	☐ Grapefruit	☐ Fruit Bars	☐ Onions
☐ _____	☐ _____	☐ _____	☐ _____	☐ _____

POST-TRIP REVIEW

To make every camping trip better, it's important to capture and review what you liked and what you would change. Use this sheet to review and plan your next adventure.

Campground Name _____ Dates _____ To _____

Address Street _____ City _____ State _____

Type of Site/Park ☐ National ☐ State ☐ Private Campsite # _____

Types of Campsite ☐ Managed/RV ☐ Primitive ☐ Boondocking ☐ Wilderness

Types of Trip ☐ Basic Camping ☐ Glamping (Tent/Rental/RV)
☐ Bushcraft ☐ Primitive ☐ Combination

Sites/Excursions Along the Way

1 _____ 2 _____ 3 _____

Designated Tent / Pad Sites? ☐ Yes ☐ No Campsite # _____

Campground Amenities

☐ Drinking Water (close/far)   ☐ Picnic   ☐ Firewood For Sale
☐ Fire Pits/Ring   ☐ Table – RV (120V 50A/30A)   ☐ Pet Friendly
☐ Tent Pads   ☐ Hookups   ☐ Nice Town
☐ BBQ Grill   ☐ Campground Store

What You Liked / What Went Well?

1 _____

2 _____

Other _____ Restrooms: Yes / No – Close / Far – Clean / Unclean – Shower / Electricity

What You Didn't Like / What Would You Change?

1 _____

2 _____

Animal Sightings _____

Biggest Surprise OR Need That The Campground Had (Or Didn't Have)? _____

Types of Activities Did You Do? (In Tent, Campsite, Campground, Local Areas, etc.)

_____

Things (activities / side trips) To Do Next Time?

_____

People You Met?

Name _____ From City/State _____ Phone/Email _____
Name _____ From City/State _____ Phone/Email _____
Name _____ From City/State _____ Phone/Email _____

Notes

_____

_____

_____

_____

_____

CAMPING TRIP PLANNING

Ready for your next great outdoor adventure? Use this worksheet to plan your trip and have the greatest "under the stars" experience possible.

What type of trip?

☐ Camping
☐ Tent Glamping
☐ Bushcraft
☐ Backpacking
☐ Combination

Why are you going?

☐ Fun
☐ Activities
☐ Alone Time
☐ Relaxation
☐ Develop and Test New Skills
☐ Others
_____

When will you go on your trip? Dates _____ to _____

Season _____ Seasonal Concerns _____

Location

City _____ ST _____ Park Name _____

Reservations Required? ☐ Yes ☐ No   ☐ Phone ☐ Web

Reservation # _____

Who is going? Name(s)

_____   _____
_____   _____

New Camping Skills and Preparation (Pitching Tent, Shelter Building, Fire Starting, Cooking, Hunting, Scavenging, Trapping, etc.) **Preparation** (Read, videos, testing, training, certification, etc.)

• Skill _____ How will you prep/test? _____
• Skill _____ How will you prep/test? _____

Special Gear/Equipment (New Type of Tent, Gas Equipment, Generator, Backpacks, Hunting, etc.)

1 _____ 2 _____ 3 _____

Gear to be purchased, rented or repaired?

1. Type of Gear _____ Purchase, rented, repaired? _____
2. Type of Gear _____ Purchase, rented, repaired? _____

How are you prepared for rain, cold, heat, wind, bugs and varmints?

Rain _____   Cold/Heat _____
Bugs _____   Varmints/Bears _____

Major Activities – What are the different activities you will do?

	Activity	Location
Day 1	_____	_____
Day 2	_____	_____
Day 3	_____	_____
Day 4	_____	_____

Nearest Emergency Room or Help

Facility_____ Address _____ Phone _____ Hours _____

Who Knows You're Gone Name _____ Phone _____ Email _____

GEAR AND EQUIPMENT CHECKLIST

This is a basic checklist for camping, glamping & bushcraft trips. There are categories and specific camping items. Put an "X" or number in the "#" column in red or blue ink. If you don't want to take an item, then strike through it (e.g. ~~Hammock~~). Once you've loaded an item, mark an X in the LD (Loaded) column. Blanks are for add-ons. **_Bolded italicized_** items are Bushcraft suggested.

Trip to _____ # Days _____

Trip Type ☐ Camp ☐ Glamp ☐ Bushcraft Dates _____

Tent/Shelter	#	LD
Tent/Hammock		
Rainfly		
Tent carpet		
Groundsheet/Tarp		
Guy Lines/Stakes		
Mallet/Hammer		
Tent Repair Kit		
Broom/Dustpan		
Sleeping system		
Sleeping Bag		
Sleeping Pad		
Blanket		
Pillow		
Inside/Outside Rug		
Sleeping Cot		
Tent Fan/Heater		
Camp Equipment		
Shelter/Canopy		
Chair		
Table		
Gear		
Backpack/Bag		
Gear Bag		
Knife/Multi-Tool		
Shovel		
Rope		
Strap/Bungee Cords		
Compass		
First Aid Kit		
Saw/Hatchet/Ax		
Duct Tape		
Work Gloves		
Activities		
Hiking/Biking Gear		

Kitchen/Cooking	#	LD
Canopy/Tarp		
Camp Kitchen		
Portable Grill/Grate		
Gas/Electric Stove & Fuel		
Dutch Oven & DO Lifter		
Pots / Pans / Skillet		
Cooler		
Table		
Water Jug		
Trash Can & Bags		
Drink/Coffee Cups		
Charcoal & Starter		
Dish/Biodegradable Soap		
Clothe & Paper Towels		
Grill Utensils/Oven Mitt		
Pots/Dishes		
Mess Kit		
Aluminum Foil		
Big Cutting Knives		
Frying Pan/Spatula		
Coffee Pot/Press/Maker		
Bottle/Wine Opener		
Wipes		
Ice		
Campfire		
Local Firewood		
Matches/Lighter/Starter		
Fire Extinguisher		
Roasting Sticks		
Electrical		
Flashlight		
Headlamp/Floodlight		
Lantern Fuel/Electric		
Extension Cord		
Extra Batteries / Charger		
Activities		
Fishing Gear / Bait		

Personal	#	LD
GUYS		
Jacket/Coat		
Shirts		
Pants		
Shorts		
Underwear		
Hygiene Kit		
Hat / Visor		
Socks		
Shoes / Boots		
Rain Gear		
Swimwear		
Sleepwear		
GIRLS		
Jacket/Coat		
Shirts/Blouses		
Pants		
Shorts		
Underwear		
Hygiene Kit		
Hat/Visor		
Socks		
Shoes/Boots		
Rain Gear		
Swimwear		
Sleepwear		
Misc		
Sunscreen/Bug Spray		
Bath Cloth/Towels		
Sunglasses		
Bandana		
Binoculars		
Activities		
Board Games/Cards		

PERSONAL ITEMS / FIRST AID

This checklist is for packing personal items for hygiene, miscellaneous, and first aid. The personal item section is designed for 4 people. To add more adults or children, just make a line to the right of the item. Use blank spaces for additional items.

Personal Item	Camper #1 ✓	#	Camper #2 ✓	#	Camper #3 ✓	#	Camper #4 ✓	#
Soap								
Toothbrush								
Toothpaste								
Dental Floss								
Deodorant								
Shampoo/Conditioner								
Comb/Brush								
Tissues								
Razor								
Shaving Cream								
Hand Sanitizer								
Cotton Tips								
Lotion								
Mouthwash								
Dental Floss								
Chapstick/Lip Balm								
Toilet Paper								
Tweezers								
Sunscreen								
Insect Repellent								
Washcloth								
Towel								
Mirror								
Hair Dryer								
Contacts/Case								
Saline Solution								
Nail Clippers/File								
Ear Plugs								
Medications								

First Aid Kit Checklist

First Aid Item	✓	#
Band Aids		
Gauze Pads		
Antiseptic Wipes		
Hydrogen Peroxide		
Cotton Balls		
Sanitizer		
Tweezers		
Scissors		
Instant Cold/Hot Packs		
Latex Gloves		
Blanket		
Oral Thermometer		
Adhesive Tape		
Antibiotic Ointment		
Antihistamines		
Crepe Bandages		
Hydrocortisone		
Painkillers		
Safety Pins		
CPR Mouthpiece		
Alcohol Wipes		
Aspirin		
Calamine Lotion		
Splint		
Sterile Eye Dressings		
Medications		
Bandana/Wraps		
First Aid Manual		

4-DAY CAMPING MEAL PLANNER

Great meals make great camping! However, preparing and cooking meals outdoors requires accurate planning to have the right ingredients and equipment for culinary success. Here is a basic meal planning guide for each meal, ingredients, cooking equipment / methods, and grocery list items. Write "Travel" for meals not needed. Use 2 Sheets For 5+Days.

	MEALS	TYPE OF MEAL/FOOD	COOKING METHOD	GROCERY ITEMS/LIST	✓
	Example	Sandwiches / Chips / Fruits	SK/None	Bread, Cold Cuts, Chips, Fruits	✓
DAY 1	Breakfast				
	Snack				
	Lunch				
	Snack				
	Dinner				
	Treat				
DAY 2	Breakfast				
	Snack				
	Lunch				
	Snack				
	Dinner				
	Treat				
DAY 3	Breakfast				
	Snack				
	Lunch				
	Snack				
	Dinner				
	Treat				
DAY 4	Breakfast				
	Snack				
	Lunch				
	Snack				
	Dinner				
	Treat				

*Cooking Methods: **(S)** Stove   **(G)** Grill   **(F)** Firepit   **(D)** Dutch Oven   **(H)** Hanging Pot   **(Sk)** Skillet

Drinks   ☐ Milk   ☐ Soda   ☐ Tea   ☐ Coffee   ☐ Drink Mix

Spices	**Condiments**	**Fruit**	**Nuts/Mix**	**Fixings**
☐ Salt	☐ Ketchup	☐ Apples	☐ Nuts/Seeds	☐ Lettuce
☐ Pepper	☐ Mustard	☐ Bananas	☐ Trail Mix	☐ Tomatoes
☐ Sugar	☐ Relish	☐ Oranges	☐ Power Bars	☐ Pickes
☐ Hot Sauce	☐ Salsa	☐ Grapefruit	☐ Fruit Bars	☐ Onions
☐ _____	☐ _____	☐ _____	☐ _____	☐ _____

POST-TRIP REVIEW

To make every camping trip better, it's important to capture and review what you liked and what you would change. Use this sheet to review and plan your next adventure.

Campground Name _____ Dates _____ To _____

Address Street _____ City _____ State _____

Type of Site/Park ☐ National ☐ State ☐ Private Campsite # _____

Types of Campsite ☐ Managed/RV ☐ Primitive ☐ Boondocking ☐ Wilderness

Types of Trip ☐ Basic Camping ☐ Glamping (Tent/Rental/RV)
☐ Bushcraft ☐ Primitive ☐ Combination

Sites/Excursions Along the Way

1 _____ 2 _____ 3 _____

Designated Tent / Pad Sites? ☐ Yes ☐ No Campsite # _____

Campground Amenities

☐ Drinking Water (close/far)   ☐ Picnic   ☐ Firewood For Sale
☐ Fire Pits/Ring   ☐ Table – RV (120V 50A/30A)   ☐ Pet Friendly
☐ Tent Pads   ☐ Hookups   ☐ Nice Town
☐ BBQ Grill   ☐ Campground Store

What You Liked / What Went Well?

1 _____
2 _____

Other _____ Restrooms: Yes / No – Close / Far – Clean / Unclean – Shower / Electricity

What You Didn't Like / What Would You Change?

1 _____
2 _____

Animal Sightings _____

Biggest Surprise OR Need That The Campground Had (Or Didn't Have)? _____

Types of Activities Did You Do? (In Tent, Campsite, Campground, Local Areas, etc.)

_____

Things (activities / side trips) To Do Next Time?

_____

People You Met?

Name _____ From City/State _____ Phone/Email _____
Name _____ From City/State _____ Phone/Email _____
Name _____ From City/State _____ Phone/Email _____

TRIP EXPERIENCES

PICTURES · MEMORIES · MAPS · MISC. · NOTES

Notes

_____

_____

_____

_____

_____

CAMPING TRIP PLANNING

Ready for your next great outdoor adventure? Use this worksheet to plan your trip and have the greatest "under the stars" experience possible.

What type of trip?

☐ Camping
☐ Tent Glamping
☐ Bushcraft
☐ Backpacking
☐ Combination

Why are you going?

☐ Fun
☐ Activities
☐ Alone Time
☐ Relaxation
☐ Develop and Test New Skills
☐ Others
_____

When will you go on your trip? Dates _____ to _____

Season _____ Seasonal Concerns _____

Location

City _____ ST _____ Park Name _____

Reservations Required? ☐ Yes ☐ No   ☐ Phone ☐ Web

Reservation # _____

Who is going? Name(s)

_____   _____
_____   _____

New Camping Skills and Preparation (Pitching Tent, Shelter Building, Fire Starting, Cooking, Hunting, Scavenging, Trapping, etc.) **Preparation** (Read, videos, testing, training, certification, etc.)

• Skill _____ How will you prep/test? _____
• Skill _____ How will you prep/test? _____

Special Gear/Equipment (New Type of Tent, Gas Equipment, Generator, Backpacks, Hunting, etc.)

1 _____   2 _____   3 _____

Gear to be purchased, rented or repaired?

1. Type of Gear _____ Purchase, rented, repaired? _____
2. Type of Gear _____ Purchase, rented, repaired? _____

How are you prepared for rain, cold, heat, wind, bugs and varmints?

Rain _____   Cold/Heat _____
Bugs _____   Varmints/Bears _____

Major Activities – What are the different activities you will do?

	Activity	Location
Day 1	_____	_____
Day 2	_____	_____
Day 3	_____	_____
Day 4	_____	_____

Nearest Emergency Room or Help

Facility_____ Address _____ Phone _____ Hours _____

Who Knows You're Gone   Name _____ Phone _____ Email _____

GEAR AND EQUIPMENT CHECKLIST

This is a basic checklist for camping, glamping & bushcraft trips. There are categories and specific camping items. Put an "X" or number in the "#" column in red or blue ink. If you don't want to take an item, then strike through it (e.g. ~~Hammock~~). Once you've loaded an item, mark an X in the LD (Loaded) column. Blanks are for add-ons. **Bolded italicized** items are Bushcraft suggested.

Trip to _____ # Days _____

Trip Type ☐ Camp   ☐ Glamp   ☐ Bushcraft   Dates _____

Tent/Shelter	#	LD
Tent/Hammock		
Rainfly		
Tent carpet		
Groundsheet/Tarp		
Guy Lines/Stakes		
Mallet/Hammer		
Tent Repair Kit		
Broom/Dustpan		
Sleeping system		
Sleeping Bag		
Sleeping Pad		
Blanket		
Pillow		
Inside/Outside Rug		
Sleeping Cot		
Tent Fan/Heater		
Camp Equipment		
Shelter/Canopy		
Chair		
Table		
Gear		
Backpack/Bag		
Gear Bag		
Knife/Multi-Tool		
Shovel		
Rope		
Strap/Bungee Cords		
Compass		
First Aid Kit		
Saw/Hatchet/Ax		
Duct Tape		
Work Gloves		
Activities		
Hiking/Biking Gear		

Kitchen/Cooking	#	LD
Canopy/Tarp		
Camp Kitchen		
Portable Grill/Grate		
Gas/Electric Stove & Fuel		
Dutch Oven & DO Lifter		
Pots / Pans / Skillet		
Cooler		
Table		
Water Jug		
Trash Can & Bags		
Drink/Coffee Cups		
Charcoal & Starter		
Dish/Biodegradable Soap		
Clothe & Paper Towels		
Grill Utensils/Oven Mitt		
Pots/Dishes		
Mess Kit		
Aluminum Foil		
Big Cutting Knives		
Frying Pan/Spatula		
Coffee Pot/Press/Maker		
Bottle/Wine Opener		
Wipes		
Ice		
Campfire		
Local Firewood		
Matches/Lighter/Starter		
Fire Extinguisher		
Roasting Sticks		
Electrical		
Flashlight		
Headlamp/Floodlight		
Lantern Fuel/Electric		
Extension Cord		
Extra Batteries / Charger		
Activities		
Fishing Gear / Bait		

Personal	#	LD
GUYS		
Jacket/Coat		
Shirts		
Pants		
Shorts		
Underwear		
Hygiene Kit		
Hat / Visor		
Socks		
Shoes / Boots		
Rain Gear		
Swimwear		
Sleepwear		
GIRLS		
Jacket/Coat		
Shirts/Blouses		
Pants		
Shorts		
Underwear		
Hygiene Kit		
Hat/Visor		
Socks		
Shoes/Boots		
Rain Gear		
Swimwear		
Sleepwear		
Misc		
Sunscreen/Bug Spray		
Bath Cloth/Towels		
Sunglasses		
Bandana		
Binoculars		
Activities		
Board Games/Cards		

PERSONAL ITEMS / FIRST AID

This checklist is for packing personal items for hygiene, miscellaneous, and first aid. The personal item section is designed for 4 people. To add more adults or children, just make a line to the right of the item. Use blank spaces for additional items.

Personal Item	Camper #1 ✓ | #	Camper #2 ✓ | #	Camper #3 ✓ | #	Camper #4 ✓ | #
Soap				
Toothbrush				
Toothpaste				
Dental Floss				
Deodorant				
Shampoo/Conditioner				
Comb/Brush				
Tissues				
Razor				
Shaving Cream				
Hand Sanitizer				
Cotton Tips				
Lotion				
Mouthwash				
Dental Floss				
Chapstick/Lip Balm				
Toilet Paper				
Tweezers				
Sunscreen				
Insect Repellent				
Washcloth				
Towel				
Mirror				
Hair Dryer				
Contacts/Case				
Saline Solution				
Nail Clippers/File				
Ear Plugs				
Medications				

First Aid Kit Checklist

First Aid Item	✓ | #
Band Aids	
Gauze Pads	
Antiseptic Wipes	
Hydrogen Peroxide	
Cotton Balls	
Sanitizer	
Tweezers	
Scissors	
Instant Cold/Hot Packs	
Latex Gloves	
Blanket	
Oral Thermometer	
Adhesive Tape	
Antibiotic Ointment	
Antihistamines	
Crepe Bandages	
Hydrocortisone	
Painkillers	
Safety Pins	
CPR Mouthpiece	
Alcohol Wipes	
Aspirin	
Calamine Lotion	
Splint	
Sterile Eye Dressings	
Medications	
Bandana/Wraps	
First Aid Manual	

4-DAY CAMPING MEAL PLANNER

Great meals make great camping! However, preparing and cooking meals outdoors requires accurate planning to have the right ingredients and equipment for culinary success. Here is a basic meal planning guide for each meal, ingredients, cooking equipment / methods, and grocery list items. Write "Travel" for meals not needed. Use 2 Sheets For 5+Days.

MEALS	TYPE OF MEAL/FOOD	COOKING METHOD	GROCERY ITEMS/LIST	✓
Example	Sandwiches / Chips / Fruits	SK/None	Bread, Cold Cuts, Chips, Fruits	✓
DAY 1 Breakfast				
Snack				
Lunch				
Snack				
Dinner				
Treat				
DAY 2 Breakfast				
Snack				
Lunch				
Snack				
Dinner				
Treat				
DAY 3 Breakfast				
Snack				
Lunch				
Snack				
Dinner				
Treat				
DAY 4 Breakfast				
Snack				
Lunch				
Snack				
Dinner				
Treat				

*Cooking Methods: **(S)** Stove **(G)** Grill **(F)** Firepit **(D)** Dutch Oven **(H)** Hanging Pot **(Sk)** Skillet

Drinks   ☐ Milk   ☐ Soda   ☐ Tea   ☐ Coffee   ☐ Drink Mix

Spices	**Condiments**	**Fruit**	**Nuts/Mix**	**Fixings**
☐ Salt	☐ Ketchup	☐ Apples	☐ Nuts/Seeds	☐ Lettuce
☐ Pepper	☐ Mustard	☐ Bananas	☐ Trail Mix	☐ Tomatoes
☐ Sugar	☐ Relish	☐ Oranges	☐ Power Bars	☐ Pickes
☐ Hot Sauce	☐ Salsa	☐ Grapefruit	☐ Fruit Bars	☐ Onions
☐ _____	☐ _____	☐ _____	☐ _____	☐ _____

POST-TRIP REVIEW

To make every camping trip better, it's important to capture and review what you liked and what you would change. Use this sheet to review and plan your next adventure.

Campground Name _____ Dates _____ To _____

Address Street _____ City _____ State _____

Type of Site/Park ☐ National ☐ State ☐ Private Campsite # _____

Types of Campsite ☐ Managed/RV ☐ Primitive ☐ Boondocking ☐ Wilderness

Types of Trip ☐ Basic Camping ☐ Glamping (Tent/Rental/RV)
 ☐ Bushcraft ☐ Primitive ☐ Combination

Sites/Excursions Along the Way

1 _____ 2 _____ 3 _____

Designated Tent / Pad Sites? ☐ Yes ☐ No Campsite # _____

Campground Amenities

☐ Drinking Water (close/far) ☐ Picnic ☐ Firewood For Sale
☐ Fire Pits/Ring ☐ Table – RV (120V 50A/30A) ☐ Pet Friendly
☐ Tent Pads ☐ Hookups ☐ Nice Town
☐ BBQ Grill ☐ Campground Store

What You Liked / What Went Well?

1 _____
2 _____

Other _____ Restrooms: Yes / No – Close / Far – Clean / Unclean – Shower / Electricity

What You Didn't Like / What Would You Change?

1 _____
2 _____

Animal Sightings _____

Biggest Surprise OR Need That The Campground Had (Or Didn't Have)?_____

Types of Activities Did You Do? (In Tent, Campsite, Campground, Local Areas, etc.)

_____

Things (activities / side trips) To Do Next Time?

_____

People You Met?

Name _____ From City/State _____ Phone/Email _____
Name _____ From City/State _____ Phone/Email _____
Name _____ From City/State _____ Phone/Email _____

Notes

_____

_____

_____

_____

_____

CAMPING TRIP PLANNING

Ready for your next great outdoor adventure? Use this worksheet to plan your trip and have the greatest "under the stars" experience possible.

What type of trip?

☐ Camping
☐ Tent Glamping
☐ Bushcraft
☐ Backpacking
☐ Combination

Why are you going?

☐ Fun
☐ Activities
☐ Alone Time
☐ Relaxation
☐ Develop and Test New Skills
☐ Others
_____

When will you go on your trip? Dates _____ to _____

Season _____ Seasonal Concerns _____

Location

City _____ ST _____ Park Name _____

Reservations Required? ☐ Yes ☐ No ☐ Phone ☐ Web

Reservation # _____

Who is going? Name(s)

_____ _____
_____ _____

New Camping Skills and Preparation (Pitching Tent, Shelter Building, Fire Starting, Cooking, Hunting, Scavenging, Trapping, etc.) **Preparation** (Read, videos, testing, training, certification, etc.)

- Skill _____ How will you prep/test? _____
- Skill _____ How will you prep/test? _____

Special Gear/Equipment (New Type of Tent, Gas Equipment, Generator, Backpacks, Hunting, etc.)

1 _____ 2 _____ 3 _____

Gear to be purchased, rented or repaired?

1. Type of Gear _____ Purchase, rented, repaired? _____
2. Type of Gear _____ Purchase, rented, repaired? _____

How are you prepared for rain, cold, heat, wind, bugs and varmints?

Rain _____   Cold/Heat _____
Bugs _____   Varmints/Bears _____

Major Activities – What are the different activities you will do?

	Activity	Location
Day 1	_____	_____
Day 2	_____	_____
Day 3	_____	_____
Day 4	_____	_____

Nearest Emergency Room or Help

Facility_____ Address _____ Phone _____ Hours _____

Who Knows You're Gone Name _____ Phone _____ Email _____

GEAR AND EQUIPMENT CHECKLIST

This is a basic checklist for camping, glamping & bushcraft trips. There are categories and specific camping items. Put an "X" or number in the "#" column in red or blue ink. If you don't want to take an item, then strike through it (e.g. ~~Hammock~~). Once you've loaded an item, mark an X in the LD (Loaded) column. Blanks are for add-ons. **Bolded italicized** items are Bushcraft suggested.

Trip to _____ # Days _____

Trip Type ☐ Camp ☐ Glamp ☐ Bushcraft Dates _____

Tent/Shelter	#	LD
Tent/Hammock		
Rainfly		
Tent carpet		
Groundsheet/Tarp		
Guy Lines/Stakes		
Mallet/Hammer		
Tent Repair Kit		
Broom/Dustpan		
Sleeping system		
Sleeping Bag		
Sleeping Pad		
Blanket		
Pillow		
Inside/Outside Rug		
Sleeping Cot		
Tent Fan/Heater		
Camp Equipment		
Shelter/Canopy		
Chair		
Table		
Gear		
Backpack/Bag		
Gear Bag		
Knife/Multi-Tool		
Shovel		
Rope		
Strap/Bungee Cords		
Compass		
First Aid Kit		
Saw/Hatchet/Ax		
Duct Tape		
Work Gloves		
Activities		
Hiking/Biking Gear		

Kitchen/Cooking	#	LD
Canopy/Tarp		
Camp Kitchen		
Portable Grill/Grate		
Gas/Electric Stove & Fuel		
Dutch Oven & DO Lifter		
Pots / Pans / Skillet		
Cooler		
Table		
Water Jug		
Trash Can & Bags		
Drink/Coffee Cups		
Charcoal & Starter		
Dish/Biodegradable Soap		
Clothe & Paper Towels		
Grill Utensils/Oven Mitt		
Pots/Dishes		
Mess Kit		
Aluminum Foil		
Big Cutting Knives		
Frying Pan/Spatula		
Coffee Pot/Press/Maker		
Bottle/Wine Opener		
Wipes		
Ice		
Campfire		
Local Firewood		
Matches/Lighter/Starter		
Fire Extinguisher		
Roasting Sticks		
Electrical		
Flashlight		
Headlamp/Floodlight		
Lantern Fuel/Electric		
Extension Cord		
Extra Batteries / Charger		
Activities		
Fishing Gear / Bait		

Personal	#	LD
GUYS		
Jacket/Coat		
Shirts		
Pants		
Shorts		
Underwear		
Hygiene Kit		
Hat / Visor		
Socks		
Shoes / Boots		
Rain Gear		
Swimwear		
Sleepwear		
GIRLS		
Jacket/Coat		
Shirts/Blouses		
Pants		
Shorts		
Underwear		
Hygiene Kit		
Hat/Visor		
Socks		
Shoes/Boots		
Rain Gear		
Swimwear		
Sleepwear		
Misc		
Sunscreen/Bug Spray		
Bath Cloth/Towels		
Sunglasses		
Bandana		
Binoculars		
Activities		
Board Games/Cards		

PERSONAL ITEMS / FIRST AID

This checklist is for packing personal items for hygiene, miscellaneous, and first aid. The personal item section is designed for 4 people. To add more adults or children, just make a line to the right of the item. Use blank spaces for additional items.

Personal Item	Camper #1 ✓ | #	Camper #2 ✓ | #	Camper #3 ✓ | #	Camper #4 ✓ | #
Soap				
Toothbrush				
Toothpaste				
Dental Floss				
Deodorant				
Shampoo/Conditioner				
Comb/Brush				
Tissues				
Razor				
Shaving Cream				
Hand Sanitizer				
Cotton Tips				
Lotion				
Mouthwash				
Dental Floss				
Chapstick/Lip Balm				
Toilet Paper				
Tweezers				
Sunscreen				
Insect Repellent				
Washcloth				
Towel				
Mirror				
Hair Dryer				
Contacts/Case				
Saline Solution				
Nail Clippers/File				
Ear Plugs				
Medications				

First Aid Kit Checklist

First Aid Item	✓ | #
Band Aids	
Gauze Pads	
Antiseptic Wipes	
Hydrogen Peroxide	
Cotton Balls	
Sanitizer	
Tweezers	
Scissors	
Instant Cold/Hot Packs	
Latex Gloves	
Blanket	
Oral Thermometer	
Adhesive Tape	
Antibiotic Ointment	
Antihistamines	
Crepe Bandages	
Hydrocortisone	
Painkillers	
Safety Pins	
CPR Mouthpiece	
Alcohol Wipes	
Aspirin	
Calamine Lotion	
Splint	
Sterile Eye Dressings	
Medications	
Bandana/Wraps	
First Aid Manual	

4-DAY CAMPING MEAL PLANNER

Great meals make great camping! However, preparing and cooking meals outdoors requires accurate planning to have the right ingredients and equipment for culinary success. Here is a basic meal planning guide for each meal, ingredients, cooking equipment / methods, and grocery list items. Write "Travel" for meals not needed. Use 2 Sheets For 5+Days.

MEALS	TYPE OF MEAL/FOOD	COOKING METHOD	GROCERY ITEMS/LIST	✓
Example	Sandwiches / Chips / Fruits	SK/None	Bread, Cold Cuts, Chips, Fruits	✓
DAY 1 Breakfast				
Snack				
Lunch				
Snack				
Dinner				
Treat				
DAY 2 Breakfast				
Snack				
Lunch				
Snack				
Dinner				
Treat				
DAY 3 Breakfast				
Snack				
Lunch				
Snack				
Dinner				
Treat				
DAY 4 Breakfast				
Snack				
Lunch				
Snack				
Dinner				
Treat				

*Cooking Methods: (S) Stove **(G)** Grill **(F)** Firepit **(D)** Dutch Oven **(H)** Hanging Pot **(Sk)** Skillet

Drinks ☐ Milk ☐ Soda ☐ Tea ☐ Coffee ☐ Drink Mix

Spices	**Condiments**	**Fruit**	**Nuts/Mix**	**Fixings**
☐ Salt	☐ Ketchup	☐ Apples	☐ Nuts/Seeds	☐ Lettuce
☐ Pepper	☐ Mustard	☐ Bananas	☐ Trail Mix	☐ Tomatoes
☐ Sugar	☐ Relish	☐ Oranges	☐ Power Bars	☐ Pickes
☐ Hot Sauce	☐ Salsa	☐ Grapefruit	☐ Fruit Bars	☐ Onions
☐ _____	☐ _____	☐ _____	☐ _____	☐ _____

POST-TRIP REVIEW

To make every camping trip better, it's important to capture and review what you liked and what you would change. Use this sheet to review and plan your next adventure.

Campground Name _____ Dates _____ To _____

Address Street _____ City _____ State _____

Type of Site/Park ☐ National ☐ State ☐ Private Campsite # _____

Types of Campsite ☐ Managed/RV ☐ Primitive ☐ Boondocking ☐ Wilderness

Types of Trip ☐ Basic Camping ☐ Glamping (Tent/Rental/RV)
☐ Bushcraft ☐ Primitive ☐ Combination

Sites/Excursions Along the Way

1 _____ 2 _____ 3 _____

Designated Tent / Pad Sites? ☐ Yes ☐ No Campsite # _____

Campground Amenities

☐ Drinking Water (close/far)   ☐ Picnic   ☐ Firewood For Sale
☐ Fire Pits/Ring   ☐ Table – RV (120V 50A/30A)   ☐ Pet Friendly
☐ Tent Pads   ☐ Hookups   ☐ Nice Town
☐ BBQ Grill   ☐ Campground Store

What You Liked / What Went Well?

1 _____

2 _____

Other _____ Restrooms: Yes / No – Close / Far – Clean / Unclean – Shower / Electricity

What You Didn't Like / What Would You Change?

1 _____

2 _____

Animal Sightings _____

Biggest Surprise OR Need That The Campground Had (Or Didn't Have)?_____

Types of Activities Did You Do? (In Tent, Campsite, Campground, Local Areas, etc.)

_____

Things (activities / side trips) To Do Next Time?

_____

People You Met?

Name _____ From City/State _____ Phone/Email _____
Name _____ From City/State _____ Phone/Email _____
Name _____ From City/State _____ Phone/Email _____

TRIP EXPERIENCES

Notes

CAMPING TRIP PLANNING

Ready for your next great outdoor adventure? Use this worksheet to plan your trip and have the greatest "under the stars" experience possible.

What type of trip?

☐ Camping
☐ Tent Glamping
☐ Bushcraft
☐ Backpacking
☐ Combination

Why are you going?

☐ Fun
☐ Activities
☐ Alone Time
☐ Relaxation
☐ Develop and Test New Skills
☐ Others
_____

When will you go on your trip? Dates _____ to _____

Season _____ Seasonal Concerns _____

Location

City _____ ST _____ Park Name _____

Reservations Required? ☐ Yes ☐ No   ☐ Phone ☐ Web

Reservation # _____

Who is going? Name(s)

_____   _____
_____   _____

New Camping Skills and Preparation (Pitching Tent, Shelter Building, Fire Starting, Cooking, Hunting, Scavenging, Trapping, etc.) **Preparation** (Read, videos, testing, training, certification, etc.)

• Skill _____ How will you prep/test? _____
• Skill _____ How will you prep/test? _____

Special Gear/Equipment (New Type of Tent, Gas Equipment, Generator, Backpacks, Hunting, etc.)

1 _____ 2 _____ 3 _____

Gear to be purchased, rented or repaired?

1. Type of Gear _____ Purchase, rented, repaired? _____
2. Type of Gear _____ Purchase, rented, repaired? _____

How are you prepared for rain, cold, heat, wind, bugs and varmints?

Rain _____   Cold/Heat _____
Bugs _____   Varmints/Bears _____

Major Activities – What are the different activities you will do?

	Activity	Location
Day 1	_____	_____
Day 2	_____	_____
Day 3	_____	_____
Day 4	_____	_____

Nearest Emergency Room or Help

Facility_____ Address _____ Phone _____ Hours _____

Who Knows You're Gone Name _____ Phone _____ Email _____

GEAR AND EQUIPMENT CHECKLIST

This is a basic checklist for camping, glamping & bushcraft trips. There are categories and specific camping items. Put an "X" or number in the "#" column in red or blue ink. If you don't want to take an item, then strike through it (e.g. ~~Hammock~~). Once you've loaded an item, mark an X in the LD (Loaded) column. Blanks are for add-ons. ***Bolded italicized*** items are Bushcraft suggested.

Trip to _____ # Days _____

Trip Type ☐ Camp ☐ Glamp ☐ Bushcraft Dates _____

Tent/Shelter	#	LD
Tent/Hammock		
Rainfly		
Tent carpet		
Groundsheet/Tarp		
Guy Lines/Stakes		
Mallet/Hammer		
Tent Repair Kit		
Broom/Dustpan		
Sleeping system		
Sleeping Bag		
Sleeping Pad		
Blanket		
Pillow		
Inside/Outside Rug		
Sleeping Cot		
Tent Fan/Heater		
Camp Equipment		
Shelter/Canopy		
Chair		
Table		
Gear		
Backpack/Bag		
Gear Bag		
Knife/Multi-Tool		
Shovel		
Rope		
Strap/Bungee Cords		
Compass		
First Aid Kit		
Saw/Hatchet/Ax		
Duct Tape		
Work Gloves		
Activities		
Hiking/Biking Gear		

Kitchen/Cooking	#	LD
Canopy/Tarp		
Camp Kitchen		
Portable Grill/Grate		
Gas/Electric Stove & Fuel		
Dutch Oven & DO Lifter		
Pots / Pans / Skillet		
Cooler		
Table		
Water Jug		
Trash Can & Bags		
Drink/Coffee Cups		
Charcoal & Starter		
Dish/Biodegradable Soap		
Clothe & Paper Towels		
Grill Utensils/Oven Mitt		
Pots/Dishes		
Mess Kit		
Aluminum Foil		
Big Cutting Knives		
Frying Pan/Spatula		
Coffee Pot/Press/Maker		
Bottle/Wine Opener		
Wipes		
Ice		
Campfire		
Local Firewood		
Matches/Lighter/Starter		
Fire Extinguisher		
Roasting Sticks		
Electrical		
Flashlight		
Headlamp/Floodlight		
Lantern Fuel/Electric		
Extension Cord		
Extra Batteries / Charger		
Activities		
Fishing Gear / Bait		

Personal	#	LD
GUYS		
Jacket/Coat		
Shirts		
Pants		
Shorts		
Underwear		
Hygiene Kit		
Hat / Visor		
Socks		
Shoes / Boots		
Rain Gear		
Swimwear		
Sleepwear		
GIRLS		
Jacket/Coat		
Shirts/Blouses		
Pants		
Shorts		
Underwear		
Hygiene Kit		
Hat/Visor		
Socks		
Shoes/Boots		
Rain Gear		
Swimwear		
Sleepwear		
Misc		
Sunscreen/Bug Spray		
Bath Cloth/Towels		
Sunglasses		
Bandana		
Binoculars		
Activities		
Board Games/Cards		

PERSONAL ITEMS / FIRST AID

This checklist is for packing personal items for hygiene, miscellaneous, and first aid. The personal item section is designed for 4 people. To add more adults or children, just make a line to the right of the item. Use blank spaces for additional items.

Personal Item	Camper #1 ✓ | #	Camper #2 ✓ | #	Camper #3 ✓ | #	Camper #4 ✓ | #
Soap				
Toothbrush				
Toothpaste				
Dental Floss				
Deodorant				
Shampoo/Conditioner				
Comb/Brush				
Tissues				
Razor				
Shaving Cream				
Hand Sanitizer				
Cotton Tips				
Lotion				
Mouthwash				
Dental Floss				
Chapstick/Lip Balm				
Toilet Paper				
Tweezers				
Sunscreen				
Insect Repellent				
Washcloth				
Towel				
Mirror				
Hair Dryer				
Contacts/Case				
Saline Solution				
Nail Clippers/File				
Ear Plugs				
Medications				

First Aid Kit Checklist

First Aid Item	✓ | #
Band Aids	
Gauze Pads	
Antiseptic Wipes	
Hydrogen Peroxide	
Cotton Balls	
Sanitizer	
Tweezers	
Scissors	
Instant Cold/Hot Packs	
Latex Gloves	
Blanket	
Oral Thermometer	
Adhesive Tape	
Antibiotic Ointment	
Antihistamines	
Crepe Bandages	
Hydrocortisone	
Painkillers	
Safety Pins	
CPR Mouthpiece	
Alcohol Wipes	
Aspirin	
Calamine Lotion	
Splint	
Sterile Eye Dressings	
Medications	
Bandana/Wraps	
First Aid Manual	

4-DAY CAMPING MEAL PLANNER

Great meals make great camping! However, preparing and cooking meals outdoors requires accurate planning to have the right ingredients and equipment for culinary success. Here is a basic meal planning guide for each meal, ingredients, cooking equipment / methods, and grocery list items. Write "Travel" for meals not needed. Use 2 Sheets For 5+Days.

MEALS	TYPE OF MEAL/FOOD	COOKING METHOD	GROCERY ITEMS/LIST	✔
Example	Sandwiches / Chips / Fruits	SK/None	Bread, Cold Cuts, Chips, Fruits	✔
DAY 1 Breakfast				
Snack				
Lunch				
Snack				
Dinner				
Treat				
DAY 2 Breakfast				
Snack				
Lunch				
Snack				
Dinner				
Treat				
DAY 3 Breakfast				
Snack				
Lunch				
Snack				
Dinner				
Treat				
DAY 4 Breakfast				
Snack				
Lunch				
Snack				
Dinner				
Treat				

*Cooking Methods: **(S)** Stove **(G)** Grill **(F)** Firepit **(D)** Dutch Oven **(H)** Hanging Pot **(Sk)** Skillet

Drinks ☐ Milk ☐ Soda ☐ Tea ☐ Coffee ☐ Drink Mix

Spices	**Condiments**	**Fruit**	**Nuts/Mix**	**Fixings**
☐ Salt	☐ Ketchup	☐ Apples	☐ Nuts/Seeds	☐ Lettuce
☐ Pepper	☐ Mustard	☐ Bananas	☐ Trail Mix	☐ Tomatoes
☐ Sugar	☐ Relish	☐ Oranges	☐ Power Bars	☐ Pickes
☐ Hot Sauce	☐ Salsa	☐ Grapefruit	☐ Fruit Bars	☐ Onions
☐ _____	☐ _____	☐ _____	☐ _____	☐ _____

POST-TRIP REVIEW

To make every camping trip better, it's important to capture and review what you liked and what you would change. Use this sheet to review and plan your next adventure.

Campground Name _____ Dates _____ To _____

Address Street _____ City _____ State _____

Type of Site/Park ☐ National ☐ State ☐ Private Campsite # _____

Types of Campsite ☐ Managed/RV ☐ Primitive ☐ Boondocking ☐ Wilderness

Types of Trip ☐ Basic Camping ☐ Glamping (Tent/Rental/RV)
☐ Bushcraft ☐ Primitive ☐ Combination

Sites/Excursions Along the Way

1 _____ 2 _____ 3 _____

Designated Tent / Pad Sites? ☐ Yes ☐ No Campsite # _____

Campground Amenities

☐ Drinking Water (close/far)
☐ Fire Pits/Ring
☐ Tent Pads
☐ BBQ Grill

☐ Picnic
☐ Table – RV (120V 50A/30A)
☐ Hookups
☐ Campground Store

☐ Firewood For Sale
☐ Pet Friendly
☐ Nice Town

What You Liked / What Went Well?

1 _____

2 _____

Other _____ Restrooms: Yes / No – Close / Far – Clean / Unclean – Shower / Electricity

What You Didn't Like / What Would You Change?

1 _____

2 _____

Animal Sightings _____

Biggest Surprise OR Need That The Campground Had (Or Didn't Have)? _____

Types of Activities Did You Do? (In Tent, Campsite, Campground, Local Areas, etc.)

_____

Things (activities / side trips) To Do Next Time?

_____

People You Met?

Name _____ From City/State _____ Phone/Email _____

Name _____ From City/State _____ Phone/Email _____

Name _____ From City/State _____ Phone/Email _____

TRIP EXPERIENCES

Notes

_____

_____

_____

_____

_____

CAMPING TRIP PLANNING

Ready for your next great outdoor adventure? Use this worksheet to plan your trip and have the greatest "under the stars" experience possible.

What type of trip?

- ☐ Camping
- ☐ Tent Glamping
- ☐ Bushcraft
- ☐ Backpacking
- ☐ Combination

Why are you going?

- ☐ Fun
- ☐ Activities
- ☐ Alone Time
- ☐ Relaxation
- ☐ Develop and Test New Skills
- ☐ Others
  _____

When will you go on your trip? Dates _____ to _____

Season _____ Seasonal Concerns _____

Location

City _____ ST _____ Park Name _____

Reservations Required? ☐ Yes ☐ No   ☐ Phone ☐ Web

Reservation # _____

Who is going? Name(s)

_____   _____
_____   _____

New Camping Skills and Preparation (Pitching Tent, Shelter Building, Fire Starting, Cooking, Hunting, Scavenging, Trapping, etc.) **Preparation** (Read, videos, testing, training, certification, etc.)

- Skill _____ How will you prep/test? _____
- Skill _____ How will you prep/test? _____

Special Gear/Equipment (New Type of Tent, Gas Equipment, Generator, Backpacks, Hunting, etc.)

1 _____   2 _____   3 _____

Gear to be purchased, rented or repaired?

1. Type of Gear _____ Purchase, rented, repaired? _____
2. Type of Gear _____ Purchase, rented, repaired? _____

How are you prepared for rain, cold, heat, wind, bugs and varmints?

Rain _____   Cold/Heat _____
Bugs _____   Varmints/Bears _____

Major Activities – What are the different activities you will do?

	Activity	Location
Day 1	_____	_____
Day 2	_____	_____
Day 3	_____	_____
Day 4	_____	_____

Nearest Emergency Room or Help

Facility_____ Address _____ Phone _____ Hours _____

Who Knows You're Gone   Name _____ Phone _____ Email _____

GEAR AND EQUIPMENT CHECKLIST

This is a basic checklist for camping, glamping & bushcraft trips. There are categories and specific camping items. Put an "X" or number in the "#" column in red or blue ink. If you don't want to take an item, then strike through it (e.g. ~~Hammock~~). Once you've loaded an item, mark an X in the LD (Loaded) column. Blanks are for add-ons. **Bolded italicized** items are Bushcraft suggested.

Trip to _____ # Days _____

Trip Type ☐ Camp   ☐ Glamp   ☐ Bushcraft   Dates _____

Tent/Shelter	#	LD
Tent/Hammock		
Rainfly		
Tent carpet		
Groundsheet/Tarp		
Guy Lines/Stakes		
Mallet/Hammer		
Tent Repair Kit		
Broom/Dustpan		
Sleeping system		
Sleeping Bag		
Sleeping Pad		
Blanket		
Pillow		
Inside/Outside Rug		
Sleeping Cot		
Tent Fan/Heater		
Camp Equipment		
Shelter/Canopy		
Chair		
Table		
Gear		
Backpack/Bag		
Gear Bag		
Knife/Multi-Tool		
Shovel		
Rope		
Strap/Bungee Cords		
Compass		
First Aid Kit		
Saw/Hatchet/Ax		
Duct Tape		
Work Gloves		
Activities		
Hiking/Biking Gear		

Kitchen/Cooking	#	LD
Canopy/Tarp		
Camp Kitchen		
Portable Grill/Grate		
Gas/Electric Stove & Fuel		
Dutch Oven & DO Lifter		
Pots / Pans / Skillet		
Cooler		
Table		
Water Jug		
Trash Can & Bags		
Drink/Coffee Cups		
Charcoal & Starter		
Dish/Biodegradable Soap		
Clothe & Paper Towels		
Grill Utensils/Oven Mitt		
Pots/Dishes		
Mess Kit		
Aluminum Foil		
Big Cutting Knives		
Frying Pan/Spatula		
Coffee Pot/Press/Maker		
Bottle/Wine Opener		
Wipes		
Ice		
Campfire		
Local Firewood		
Matches/Lighter/Starter		
Fire Extinguisher		
Roasting Sticks		
Electrical		
Flashlight		
Headlamp/Floodlight		
Lantern Fuel/Electric		
Extension Cord		
Extra Batteries / Charger		
Activities		
Fishing Gear / Bait		

Personal	#	LD
GUYS		
Jacket/Coat		
Shirts		
Pants		
Shorts		
Underwear		
Hygiene Kit		
Hat / Visor		
Socks		
Shoes / Boots		
Rain Gear		
Swimwear		
Sleepwear		
GIRLS		
Jacket/Coat		
Shirts/Blouses		
Pants		
Shorts		
Underwear		
Hygiene Kit		
Hat/Visor		
Socks		
Shoes/Boots		
Rain Gear		
Swimwear		
Sleepwear		
Misc		
Sunscreen/Bug Spray		
Bath Cloth/Towels		
Sunglasses		
Bandana		
Binoculars		
Activities		
Board Games/Cards		

PERSONAL ITEMS / FIRST AID

This checklist is for packing personal items for hygiene, miscellaneous, and first aid. The personal item section is designed for 4 people. To add more adults or children, just make a line to the right of the item. Use blank spaces for additional items.

Personal Item	Camper #1 ✓ | #	Camper #2 ✓ | #	Camper #3 ✓ | #	Camper #4 ✓ | #
Soap				
Toothbrush				
Toothpaste				
Dental Floss				
Deodorant				
Shampoo/Conditioner				
Comb/Brush				
Tissues				
Razor				
Shaving Cream				
Hand Sanitizer				
Cotton Tips				
Lotion				
Mouthwash				
Dental Floss				
Chapstick/Lip Balm				
Toilet Paper				
Tweezers				
Sunscreen				
Insect Repellent				
Washcloth				
Towel				
Mirror				
Hair Dryer				
Contacts/Case				
Saline Solution				
Nail Clippers/File				
Ear Plugs				
Medications				

First Aid Kit Checklist

First Aid Item	✓ | #
Band Aids	
Gauze Pads	
Antiseptic Wipes	
Hydrogen Peroxide	
Cotton Balls	
Sanitizer	
Tweezers	
Scissors	
Instant Cold/Hot Packs	
Latex Gloves	
Blanket	
Oral Thermometer	
Adhesive Tape	
Antibiotic Ointment	
Antihistamines	
Crepe Bandages	
Hydrocortisone	
Painkillers	
Safety Pins	
CPR Mouthpiece	
Alcohol Wipes	
Aspirin	
Calamine Lotion	
Splint	
Sterile Eye Dressings	
Medications	
Bandana/Wraps	
First Aid Manual	

4-DAY CAMPING MEAL PLANNER

Great meals make great camping! However, preparing and cooking meals outdoors requires accurate planning to have the right ingredients and equipment for culinary success. Here is a basic meal planning guide for each meal, ingredients, cooking equipment / methods, and grocery list items. Write "Travel" for meals not needed. Use 2 Sheets For 5+Days.

MEALS	TYPE OF MEAL/FOOD	COOKING METHOD	GROCERY ITEMS/LIST	✓
Example	Sandwiches / Chips / Fruits	SK/None	Bread, Cold Cuts, Chips, Fruits	✓
DAY 1 Breakfast				
Snack				
Lunch				
Snack				
Dinner				
Treat				
DAY 2 Breakfast				
Snack				
Lunch				
Snack				
Dinner				
Treat				
DAY 3 Breakfast				
Snack				
Lunch				
Snack				
Dinner				
Treat				
DAY 4 Breakfast				
Snack				
Lunch				
Snack				
Dinner				
Treat				

*Cooking Methods: **(S)** Stove   **(G)** Grill   **(F)** Firepit   **(D)** Dutch Oven   **(H)** Hanging Pot   **(Sk)** Skillet

Drinks   ☐ Milk   ☐ Soda   ☐ Tea   ☐ Coffee   ☐ Drink Mix

Spices	**Condiments**	**Fruit**	**Nuts/Mix**	**Fixings**
☐ Salt	☐ Ketchup	☐ Apples	☐ Nuts/Seeds	☐ Lettuce
☐ Pepper	☐ Mustard	☐ Bananas	☐ Trail Mix	☐ Tomatoes
☐ Sugar	☐ Relish	☐ Oranges	☐ Power Bars	☐ Pickes
☐ Hot Sauce	☐ Salsa	☐ Grapefruit	☐ Fruit Bars	☐ Onions
☐ _____	☐ _____	☐ _____	☐ _____	☐ _____

POST-TRIP REVIEW

To make every camping trip better, it's important to capture and review what you liked and what you would change. Use this sheet to review and plan your next adventure.

Campground Name _____ Dates _____ To _____

Address Street _____ City _____ State _____

Type of Site/Park ☐ National   ☐ State   ☐ Private   Campsite # _____

Types of Campsite ☐ Managed/RV   ☐ Primitive   ☐ Boondocking   ☐ Wilderness

Types of Trip ☐ Basic Camping   ☐ Glamping (Tent/Rental/RV)
☐ Bushcraft   ☐ Primitive   ☐ Combination

Sites/Excursions Along the Way

1 _____ 2 _____ 3 _____

Designated Tent / Pad Sites?   ☐ Yes   ☐ No   Campsite # _____

Campground Amenities

☐ Drinking Water (close/far)   ☐ Picnic   ☐ Firewood For Sale
☐ Fire Pits/Ring   ☐ Table – RV (120V 50A/30A)   ☐ Pet Friendly
☐ Tent Pads   ☐ Hookups   ☐ Nice Town
☐ BBQ Grill   ☐ Campground Store

What You Liked / What Went Well?

1 _____

2 _____

Other _____ Restrooms: Yes / No – Close / Far – Clean / Unclean – Shower / Electricity

What You Didn't Like / What Would You Change?

1 _____

2 _____

Animal Sightings _____

Biggest Surprise OR Need That The Campground Had (Or Didn't Have)?_____

Types of Activities Did You Do? (In Tent, Campsite, Campground, Local Areas, etc.)

_____

Things (activities / side trips) To Do Next Time?

_____

People You Met?

Name _____ From City/State _____ Phone/Email _____
Name _____ From City/State _____ Phone/Email _____
Name _____ From City/State _____ Phone/Email _____

TRIP EXPERIENCES

PICTURES · MEMORIES · MAPS · MISC. · NOTES

Notes

_____

_____

_____

_____

_____

CAMPING TRIP PLANNING

Ready for your next great outdoor adventure? Use this worksheet to plan your trip and have the greatest "under the stars" experience possible.

What type of trip?

☐ Camping
☐ Tent Glamping
☐ Bushcraft
☐ Backpacking
☐ Combination

Why are you going?

☐ Fun
☐ Activities
☐ Alone Time
☐ Relaxation
☐ Develop and Test New Skills
☐ Others
_____

When will you go on your trip? Dates _____ to _____

Season _____ Seasonal Concerns _____

Location

City _____ ST _____ Park Name _____

Reservations Required? ☐ Yes ☐ No   ☐ Phone ☐ Web

Reservation # _____

Who is going? Name(s)

_____   _____

_____   _____

New Camping Skills and Preparation (Pitching Tent, Shelter Building, Fire Starting, Cooking, Hunting, Scavenging, Trapping, etc.) **Preparation** (Read, videos, testing, training, certification, etc.)

• Skill _____ How will you prep/test? _____
• Skill _____ How will you prep/test? _____

Special Gear/Equipment (New Type of Tent, Gas Equipment, Generator, Backpacks, Hunting, etc.)

1 _____   2 _____   3 _____

Gear to be purchased, rented or repaired?

1. Type of Gear _____ Purchase, rented, repaired? _____
2. Type of Gear _____ Purchase, rented, repaired? _____

How are you prepared for rain, cold, heat, wind, bugs and varmints?

Rain _____   Cold/Heat _____

Bugs _____   Varmints/Bears _____

Major Activities – What are the different activities you will do?

	Activity	Location
Day 1	_____	_____
Day 2	_____	_____
Day 3	_____	_____
Day 4	_____	_____

Nearest Emergency Room or Help

Facility_____ Address _____ Phone _____ Hours _____

Who Knows You're Gone Name _____ Phone _____ Email _____

GEAR AND EQUIPMENT CHECKLIST

This is a basic checklist for camping, glamping & bushcraft trips. There are categories and specific camping items. Put an "X" or number in the "#" column in red or blue ink. If you don't want to take an item, then strike through it (e.g. ~~Hammock~~). Once you've loaded an item, mark an X in the LD (Loaded) column. Blanks are for add-ons. **Bolded italicized** items are Bushcraft suggested.

Trip to _____ # Days _____

Trip Type ☐ Camp   ☐ Glamp   ☐ Bushcraft   Dates _____

Tent/Shelter	#	LD
Tent/Hammock		
Rainfly		
Tent carpet		
Groundsheet/Tarp		
Guy Lines/Stakes		
Mallet/Hammer		
Tent Repair Kit		
Broom/Dustpan		
Sleeping system		
Sleeping Bag		
Sleeping Pad		
Blanket		
Pillow		
Inside/Outside Rug		
Sleeping Cot		
Tent Fan/Heater		
Camp Equipment		
Shelter/Canopy		
Chair		
Table		
Gear		
Backpack/Bag		
Gear Bag		
Knife/Multi-Tool		
Shovel		
Rope		
Strap/Bungee Cords		
Compass		
First Aid Kit		
Saw/Hatchet/Ax		
Duct Tape		
Work Gloves		
Activities		
Hiking/Biking Gear		

Kitchen/Cooking	#	LD
Canopy/Tarp		
Camp Kitchen		
Portable Grill/Grate		
Gas/Electric Stove & Fuel		
Dutch Oven & DO Lifter		
Pots / Pans / Skillet		
Cooler		
Table		
Water Jug		
Trash Can & Bags		
Drink/Coffee Cups		
Charcoal & Starter		
Dish/Biodegradable Soap		
Clothe & Paper Towels		
Grill Utensils/Oven Mitt		
Pots/Dishes		
Mess Kit		
Aluminum Foil		
Big Cutting Knives		
Frying Pan/Spatula		
Coffee Pot/Press/Maker		
Bottle/Wine Opener		
Wipes		
Ice		
Campfire		
Local Firewood		
Matches/Lighter/Starter		
Fire Extinguisher		
Roasting Sticks		
Electrical		
Flashlight		
Headlamp/Floodlight		
Lantern Fuel/Electric		
Extension Cord		
Extra Batteries / Charger		
Activities		
Fishing Gear / Bait		

Personal	#	LD
GUYS		
Jacket/Coat		
Shirts		
Pants		
Shorts		
Underwear		
Hygiene Kit		
Hat / Visor		
Socks		
Shoes / Boots		
Rain Gear		
Swimwear		
Sleepwear		
GIRLS		
Jacket/Coat		
Shirts/Blouses		
Pants		
Shorts		
Underwear		
Hygiene Kit		
Hat/Visor		
Socks		
Shoes/Boots		
Rain Gear		
Swimwear		
Sleepwear		
Misc		
Sunscreen/Bug Spray		
Bath Cloth/Towels		
Sunglasses		
Bandana		
Binoculars		
Activities		
Board Games/Cards		

PERSONAL ITEMS / FIRST AID

This checklist is for packing personal items for hygiene, miscellaneous, and first aid. The personal item section is designed for 4 people. To add more adults or children, just make a line to the right of the item. Use blank spaces for additional items.

Personal Item	Camper #1 ✓ | #	Camper #2 ✓ | #	Camper #3 ✓ | #	Camper #4 ✓ | #
Soap				
Toothbrush				
Toothpaste				
Dental Floss				
Deodorant				
Shampoo/Conditioner				
Comb/Brush				
Tissues				
Razor				
Shaving Cream				
Hand Sanitizer				
Cotton Tips				
Lotion				
Mouthwash				
Dental Floss				
Chapstick/Lip Balm				
Toilet Paper				
Tweezers				
Sunscreen				
Insect Repellent				
Washcloth				
Towel				
Mirror				
Hair Dryer				
Contacts/Case				
Saline Solution				
Nail Clippers/File				
Ear Plugs				
Medications				

First Aid Kit Checklist

First Aid Item	✓ | #
Band Aids	
Gauze Pads	
Antiseptic Wipes	
Hydrogen Peroxide	
Cotton Balls	
Sanitizer	
Tweezers	
Scissors	
Instant Cold/Hot Packs	
Latex Gloves	
Blanket	
Oral Thermometer	
Adhesive Tape	
Antibiotic Ointment	
Antihistamines	
Crepe Bandages	
Hydrocortisone	
Painkillers	
Safety Pins	
CPR Mouthpiece	
Alcohol Wipes	
Aspirin	
Calamine Lotion	
Splint	
Sterile Eye Dressings	
Medications	
Bandana/Wraps	
First Aid Manual	

4-DAY CAMPING MEAL PLANNER

Great meals make great camping! However, preparing and cooking meals outdoors requires accurate planning to have the right ingredients and equipment for culinary success. Here is a basic meal planning guide for each meal, ingredients, cooking equipment / methods, and grocery list items. Write "Travel" for meals not needed. Use 2 Sheets For 5+Days.

MEALS	TYPE OF MEAL/FOOD	COOKING METHOD	GROCERY ITEMS/LIST	✓
Example	Sandwiches / Chips / Fruits	SK/None	Bread, Cold Cuts, Chips, Fruits	✓
DAY 1 Breakfast				
Snack				
Lunch				
Snack				
Dinner				
Treat				
DAY 2 Breakfast				
Snack				
Lunch				
Snack				
Dinner				
Treat				
DAY 3 Breakfast				
Snack				
Lunch				
Snack				
Dinner				
Treat				
DAY 4 Breakfast				
Snack				
Lunch				
Snack				
Dinner				
Treat				

*Cooking Methods: **(S)** Stove   **(G)** Grill   **(F)** Firepit   **(D)** Dutch Oven   **(H)** Hanging Pot   **(Sk)** Skillet

Drinks   ☐ Milk   ☐ Soda   ☐ Tea   ☐ Coffee   ☐ Drink Mix

Spices	**Condiments**	**Fruit**	**Nuts/Mix**	**Fixings**
☐ Salt	☐ Ketchup	☐ Apples	☐ Nuts/Seeds	☐ Lettuce
☐ Pepper	☐ Mustard	☐ Bananas	☐ Trail Mix	☐ Tomatoes
☐ Sugar	☐ Relish	☐ Oranges	☐ Power Bars	☐ Pickes
☐ Hot Sauce	☐ Salsa	☐ Grapefruit	☐ Fruit Bars	☐ Onions
☐ _____	☐ _____	☐ _____	☐ _____	☐ _____

POST-TRIP REVIEW

To make every camping trip better, it's important to capture and review what you liked and what you would change. Use this sheet to review and plan your next adventure.

Campground Name _____ Dates _____ To _____

Address Street _____ City _____ State _____

Type of Site/Park ☐ National ☐ State ☐ Private Campsite # _____

Types of Campsite ☐ Managed/RV ☐ Primitive ☐ Boondocking ☐ Wilderness

Types of Trip ☐ Basic Camping ☐ Glamping (Tent/Rental/RV)
                ☐ Bushcraft ☐ Primitive ☐ Combination

Sites/Excursions Along the Way

1 _____ 2 _____ 3 _____

Designated Tent / Pad Sites? ☐ Yes ☐ No Campsite # _____

Campground Amenities

☐ Drinking Water (close/far) ☐ Picnic ☐ Firewood For Sale
☐ Fire Pits/Ring ☐ Table – RV (120V 50A/30A) ☐ Pet Friendly
☐ Tent Pads ☐ Hookups ☐ Nice Town
☐ BBQ Grill ☐ Campground Store

What You Liked / What Went Well?

1 _____

2 _____

Other _____ Restrooms: Yes / No – Close / Far – Clean / Unclean – Shower / Electricity

What You Didn't Like / What Would You Change?

1 _____

2 _____

Animal Sightings _____

Biggest Surprise OR Need That The Campground Had (Or Didn't Have)? _____

Types of Activities Did You Do? (In Tent, Campsite, Campground, Local Areas, etc.)

_____

Things (activities / side trips) To Do Next Time?

_____

People You Met?

Name _____ From City/State _____ Phone/Email _____
Name _____ From City/State _____ Phone/Email _____
Name _____ From City/State _____ Phone/Email _____

TRIP EXPERIENCES

Notes

_____

_____

_____

_____

_____

CAMPING TRIP PLANNING

Ready for your next great outdoor adventure? Use this worksheet to plan your trip and have the greatest "under the stars" experience possible.

What type of trip?

- ☐ Camping
- ☐ Tent Glamping
- ☐ Bushcraft
- ☐ Backpacking
- ☐ Combination

Why are you going?

- ☐ Fun
- ☐ Activities
- ☐ Alone Time
- ☐ Relaxation
- ☐ Develop and Test New Skills
- ☐ Others
  _____

When will you go on your trip? Dates _____ to _____

Season _____ Seasonal Concerns _____

Location

City _____ ST _____ Park Name _____

Reservations Required? ☐ Yes ☐ No   ☐ Phone ☐ Web

Reservation # _____

Who is going? Name(s)

_____   _____

_____   _____

New Camping Skills and Preparation (Pitching Tent, Shelter Building, Fire Starting, Cooking, Hunting, Scavenging, Trapping, etc.) **Preparation** (Read, videos, testing, training, certification, etc.)

- Skill _____ How will you prep/test? _____
- Skill _____ How will you prep/test? _____

Special Gear/Equipment (New Type of Tent, Gas Equipment, Generator, Backpacks, Hunting, etc.)

1 _____   2 _____   3 _____

Gear to be purchased, rented or repaired?

1. Type of Gear _____ Purchase, rented, repaired? _____
2. Type of Gear _____ Purchase, rented, repaired? _____

How are you prepared for rain, cold, heat, wind, bugs and varmints?

Rain _____   Cold/Heat _____

Bugs _____   Varmints/Bears _____

Major Activities – What are the different activities you will do?

	Activity	Location
Day 1	_____	_____
Day 2	_____	_____
Day 3	_____	_____
Day 4	_____	_____

Nearest Emergency Room or Help

Facility_____ Address _____ Phone _____ Hours _____

Who Knows You're Gone   Name _____ Phone _____ Email _____

GEAR AND EQUIPMENT CHECKLIST

This is a basic checklist for camping, glamping & bushcraft trips. There are categories and specific camping items. Put an "X" or number in the "#" column in red or blue ink. If you don't want to take an item, then strike through it (e.g. ~~Hammock~~). Once you've loaded an item, mark an X in the LD (Loaded) column. Blanks are for add-ons. **_Bolded italicized_** items are Bushcraft suggested.

Trip to _____ # Days _____

Trip Type ☐ Camp ☐ Glamp ☐ Bushcraft Dates _____

Tent/Shelter	#	LD
Tent/Hammock		
Rainfly		
Tent carpet		
Groundsheet/Tarp		
Guy Lines/Stakes		
Mallet/Hammer		
Tent Repair Kit		
Broom/Dustpan		
Sleeping system		
Sleeping Bag		
Sleeping Pad		
Blanket		
Pillow		
Inside/Outside Rug		
Sleeping Cot		
Tent Fan/Heater		
Camp Equipment		
Shelter/Canopy		
Chair		
Table		
Gear		
Backpack/Bag		
Gear Bag		
Knife/Multi-Tool		
Shovel		
Rope		
Strap/Bungee Cords		
Compass		
First Aid Kit		
Saw/Hatchet/Ax		
Duct Tape		
Work Gloves		
Activities		
Hiking/Biking Gear		

Kitchen/Cooking	#	LD
Canopy/Tarp		
Camp Kitchen		
Portable Grill/Grate		
Gas/Electric Stove & Fuel		
Dutch Oven & DO Lifter		
Pots / Pans / Skillet		
Cooler		
Table		
Water Jug		
Trash Can & Bags		
Drink/Coffee Cups		
Charcoal & Starter		
Dish/Biodegradable Soap		
Clothe & Paper Towels		
Grill Utensils/Oven Mitt		
Pots/Dishes		
Mess Kit		
Aluminum Foil		
Big Cutting Knives		
Frying Pan/Spatula		
Coffee Pot/Press/Maker		
Bottle/Wine Opener		
Wipes		
Ice		
Campfire		
Local Firewood		
Matches/Lighter/Starter		
Fire Extinguisher		
Roasting Sticks		
Electrical		
Flashlight		
Headlamp/ Floodlight		
Lantern Fuel/Electric		
Extension Cord		
Extra Batteries / Charger		
Activities		
Fishing Gear / Bait		

Personal	#	LD
GUYS		
Jacket/Coat		
Shirts		
Pants		
Shorts		
Underwear		
Hygiene Kit		
Hat / Visor		
Socks		
Shoes / Boots		
Rain Gear		
Swimwear		
Sleepwear		
GIRLS		
Jacket/Coat		
Shirts/Blouses		
Pants		
Shorts		
Underwear		
Hygiene Kit		
Hat/Visor		
Socks		
Shoes/Boots		
Rain Gear		
Swimwear		
Sleepwear		
Misc		
Sunscreen/Bug Spray		
Bath Cloth/Towels		
Sunglasses		
Bandana		
Binoculars		
Activities		
Board Games/Cards		

PERSONAL ITEMS / FIRST AID

This checklist is for packing personal items for hygiene, miscellaneous, and first aid. The personal item section is designed for 4 people. To add more adults or children, just make a line to the right of the item. Use blank spaces for additional items.

Personal Item	Camper #1 ✓ | #	Camper #2 ✓ | #	Camper #3 ✓ | #	Camper #4 ✓ | #
Soap				
Toothbrush				
Toothpaste				
Dental Floss				
Deodorant				
Shampoo/Conditioner				
Comb/Brush				
Tissues				
Razor				
Shaving Cream				
Hand Sanitizer				
Cotton Tips				
Lotion				
Mouthwash				
Dental Floss				
Chapstick/Lip Balm				
Toilet Paper				
Tweezers				
Sunscreen				
Insect Repellent				
Washcloth				
Towel				
Mirror				
Hair Dryer				
Contacts/Case				
Saline Solution				
Nail Clippers/File				
Ear Plugs				
Medications				

First Aid Kit Checklist

First Aid Item	✓ | #
Band Aids	
Gauze Pads	
Antiseptic Wipes	
Hydrogen Peroxide	
Cotton Balls	
Sanitizer	
Tweezers	
Scissors	
Instant Cold/Hot Packs	
Latex Gloves	
Blanket	
Oral Thermometer	
Adhesive Tape	
Antibiotic Ointment	
Antihistamines	
Crepe Bandages	
Hydrocortisone	
Painkillers	
Safety Pins	
CPR Mouthpiece	
Alcohol Wipes	
Aspirin	
Calamine Lotion	
Splint	
Sterile Eye Dressings	
Medications	
Bandana/Wraps	
First Aid Manual	

4-DAY CAMPING MEAL PLANNER

Great meals make great camping! However, preparing and cooking meals outdoors requires accurate planning to have the right ingredients and equipment for culinary success. Here is a basic meal planning guide for each meal, ingredients, cooking equipment / methods, and grocery list items. Write "Travel" for meals not needed. Use 2 Sheets For 5+Days.

MEALS	TYPE OF MEAL/FOOD	COOKING METHOD	GROCERY ITEMS/LIST	✓
Example	Sandwiches / Chips / Fruits	SK/None	Bread, Cold Cuts, Chips, Fruits	✓
DAY 1 Breakfast				
Snack				
Lunch				
Snack				
Dinner				
Treat				
DAY 2 Breakfast				
Snack				
Lunch				
Snack				
Dinner				
Treat				
DAY 3 Breakfast				
Snack				
Lunch				
Snack				
Dinner				
Treat				
DAY 4 Breakfast				
Snack				
Lunch				
Snack				
Dinner				
Treat				

*Cooking Methods: **(S)** Stove   **(G)** Grill   **(F)** Firepit   **(D)** Dutch Oven   **(H)** Hanging Pot   **(Sk)** Skillet

Drinks   ☐ Milk   ☐ Soda   ☐ Tea   ☐ Coffee   ☐ Drink Mix

Spices	**Condiments**	**Fruit**	**Nuts/Mix**	**Fixings**
☐ Salt	☐ Ketchup	☐ Apples	☐ Nuts/Seeds	☐ Lettuce
☐ Pepper	☐ Mustard	☐ Bananas	☐ Trail Mix	☐ Tomatoes
☐ Sugar	☐ Relish	☐ Oranges	☐ Power Bars	☐ Pickes
☐ Hot Sauce	☐ Salsa	☐ Grapefruit	☐ Fruit Bars	☐ Onions
☐ _____	☐ _____	☐ _____	☐ _____	☐ _____

POST-TRIP REVIEW

To make every camping trip better, it's important to capture and review what you liked and what you would change. Use this sheet to review and plan your next adventure.

Campground Name _____ Dates _____ To _____

Address Street _____ City _____ State _____

Type of Site/Park ☐ National ☐ State ☐ Private Campsite # _____

Types of Campsite ☐ Managed/RV ☐ Primitive ☐ Boondocking ☐ Wilderness

Types of Trip ☐ Basic Camping ☐ Glamping (Tent/Rental/RV)
☐ Bushcraft ☐ Primitive ☐ Combination

Sites/Excursions Along the Way

1 _____ 2 _____ 3 _____

Designated Tent / Pad Sites? ☐ Yes ☐ No Campsite # _____

Campground Amenities

☐ Drinking Water (close/far)   ☐ Picnic   ☐ Firewood For Sale
☐ Fire Pits/Ring   ☐ Table – RV (120V 50A/30A)   ☐ Pet Friendly
☐ Tent Pads   ☐ Hookups   ☐ Nice Town
☐ BBQ Grill   ☐ Campground Store

What You Liked / What Went Well?

1 _____
2 _____

Other _____ Restrooms: Yes / No – Close / Far – Clean / Unclean – Shower / Electricity

What You Didn't Like / What Would You Change?

1 _____
2 _____

Animal Sightings _____

Biggest Surprise OR Need That The Campground Had (Or Didn't Have)? _____

Types of Activities Did You Do? (In Tent, Campsite, Campground, Local Areas, etc.)

_____

Things (activities / side trips) To Do Next Time?

_____

People You Met?

Name _____ From City/State _____ Phone/Email _____
Name _____ From City/State _____ Phone/Email _____
Name _____ From City/State _____ Phone/Email _____

TRIP EXPERIENCES

PICTURES · MEMORIES · MAPS · MISC. · NOTES

Notes

_____

_____

_____

_____

_____

CAMPING TRIP PLANNING

Ready for your next great outdoor adventure? Use this worksheet to plan your trip and have the greatest "under the stars" experience possible.

What type of trip?

☐ Camping
☐ Tent Glamping
☐ Bushcraft
☐ Backpacking
☐ Combination

Why are you going?

☐ Fun
☐ Activities
☐ Alone Time
☐ Relaxation
☐ Develop and Test New Skills
☐ Others
_____

When will you go on your trip? Dates _____ to _____

Season _____ Seasonal Concerns _____

Location

City _____ ST _____ Park Name _____

Reservations Required? ☐ Yes ☐ No   ☐ Phone ☐ Web

Reservation # _____

Who is going? Name(s)

_____   _____
_____   _____

New Camping Skills and Preparation (Pitching Tent, Shelter Building, Fire Starting, Cooking, Hunting, Scavenging, Trapping, etc.) **Preparation** (Read, videos, testing, training, certification, etc.)

• Skill _____ How will you prep/test? _____
• Skill _____ How will you prep/test? _____

Special Gear/Equipment (New Type of Tent, Gas Equipment, Generator, Backpacks, Hunting, etc.)

1 _____   2 _____   3 _____

Gear to be purchased, rented or repaired?

1. Type of Gear _____ Purchase, rented, repaired? _____
2. Type of Gear _____ Purchase, rented, repaired? _____

How are you prepared for rain, cold, heat, wind, bugs and varmints?

Rain _____   Cold/Heat _____
Bugs _____   Varmints/Bears _____

Major Activities – What are the different activities you will do?

	Activity	Location
Day 1	_____	_____
Day 2	_____	_____
Day 3	_____	_____
Day 4	_____	_____

Nearest Emergency Room or Help

Facility_____ Address _____ Phone _____ Hours _____

Who Knows You're Gone Name _____ Phone _____ Email _____

GEAR AND EQUIPMENT CHECKLIST

This is a basic checklist for camping, glamping & bushcraft trips. There are categories and specific camping items. Put an "X" or number in the "#" column in red or blue ink. If you don't want to take an item, then strike through it (e.g. ~~Hammock~~). Once you've loaded an item, mark an X in the LD (Loaded) column. Blanks are for add-ons. **Bolded italicized** items are Bushcraft suggested.

Trip to _____ # Days _____

Trip Type ☐ Camp ☐ Glamp ☐ Bushcraft Dates _____

Tent/Shelter	#	LD
Tent/Hammock		
Rainfly		
Tent carpet		
Groundsheet/Tarp		
Guy Lines/Stakes		
Mallet/Hammer		
Tent Repair Kit		
Broom/Dustpan		
Sleeping system		
Sleeping Bag		
Sleeping Pad		
Blanket		
Pillow		
Inside/Outside Rug		
Sleeping Cot		
Tent Fan/Heater		
Camp Equipment		
Shelter/Canopy		
Chair		
Table		
Gear		
Backpack/Bag		
Gear Bag		
Knife/Multi-Tool		
Shovel		
Rope		
Strap/Bungee Cords		
Compass		
First Aid Kit		
Saw/Hatchet/Ax		
Duct Tape		
Work Gloves		
Activities		
Hiking/Biking Gear		

Kitchen/Cooking	#	LD
Canopy/Tarp		
Camp Kitchen		
Portable Grill/Grate		
Gas/Electric Stove & Fuel		
Dutch Oven & DO Lifter		
Pots / Pans / Skillet		
Cooler		
Table		
Water Jug		
Trash Can & Bags		
Drink/Coffee Cups		
Charcoal & Starter		
Dish/Biodegradable Soap		
Clothe & Paper Towels		
Grill Utensils/Oven Mitt		
Pots/Dishes		
Mess Kit		
Aluminum Foil		
Big Cutting Knives		
Frying Pan/Spatula		
Coffee Pot/Press/Maker		
Bottle/Wine Opener		
Wipes		
Ice		
Campfire		
Local Firewood		
Matches/Lighter/Starter		
Fire Extinguisher		
Roasting Sticks		
Electrical		
Flashlight		
Headlamp/Floodlight		
Lantern Fuel/Electric		
Extension Cord		
Extra Batteries / Charger		
Activities		
Fishing Gear / Bait		

Personal	#	LD
GUYS		
Jacket/Coat		
Shirts		
Pants		
Shorts		
Underwear		
Hygiene Kit		
Hat / Visor		
Socks		
Shoes / Boots		
Rain Gear		
Swimwear		
Sleepwear		
GIRLS		
Jacket/Coat		
Shirts/Blouses		
Pants		
Shorts		
Underwear		
Hygiene Kit		
Hat/Visor		
Socks		
Shoes/Boots		
Rain Gear		
Swimwear		
Sleepwear		
Misc		
Sunscreen/Bug Spray		
Bath Cloth/Towels		
Sunglasses		
Bandana		
Binoculars		
Activities		
Board Games/Cards		

PERSONAL ITEMS / FIRST AID

This checklist is for packing personal items for hygiene, miscellaneous, and first aid. The personal item section is designed for 4 people. To add more adults or children, just make a line to the right of the item. Use blank spaces for additional items.

Personal Item	Camper #1 ✓ | #	Camper #2 ✓ | #	Camper #3 ✓ | #	Camper #4 ✓ | #
Soap				
Toothbrush				
Toothpaste				
Dental Floss				
Deodorant				
Shampoo/Conditioner				
Comb/Brush				
Tissues				
Razor				
Shaving Cream				
Hand Sanitizer				
Cotton Tips				
Lotion				
Mouthwash				
Dental Floss				
Chapstick/Lip Balm				
Toilet Paper				
Tweezers				
Sunscreen				
Insect Repellent				
Washcloth				
Towel				
Mirror				
Hair Dryer				
Contacts/Case				
Saline Solution				
Nail Clippers/File				
Ear Plugs				
Medications				

First Aid Kit Checklist

First Aid Item	✓ | #
Band Aids	
Gauze Pads	
Antiseptic Wipes	
Hydrogen Peroxide	
Cotton Balls	
Sanitizer	
Tweezers	
Scissors	
Instant Cold/Hot Packs	
Latex Gloves	
Blanket	
Oral Thermometer	
Adhesive Tape	
Antibiotic Ointment	
Antihistamines	
Crepe Bandages	
Hydrocortisone	
Painkillers	
Safety Pins	
CPR Mouthpiece	
Alcohol Wipes	
Aspirin	
Calamine Lotion	
Splint	
Sterile Eye Dressings	
Medications	
Bandana/Wraps	
First Aid Manual	

4-DAY CAMPING MEAL PLANNER

Great meals make great camping! However, preparing and cooking meals outdoors requires accurate planning to have the right ingredients and equipment for culinary success. Here is a basic meal planning guide for each meal, ingredients, cooking equipment / methods, and grocery list items. Write "Travel" for meals not needed. Use 2 Sheets For 5+Days.

MEALS	TYPE OF MEAL/FOOD	COOKING METHOD	GROCERY ITEMS/LIST	✓
Example	Sandwiches / Chips / Fruits	SK/None	Bread, Cold Cuts, Chips, Fruits	✓
DAY 1 Breakfast				
Snack				
Lunch				
Snack				
Dinner				
Treat				
DAY 2 Breakfast				
Snack				
Lunch				
Snack				
Dinner				
Treat				
DAY 3 Breakfast				
Snack				
Lunch				
Snack				
Dinner				
Treat				
DAY 4 Breakfast				
Snack				
Lunch				
Snack				
Dinner				
Treat				

*Cooking Methods: **(S)** Stove   **(G)** Grill   **(F)** Firepit   **(D)** Dutch Oven   **(H)** Hanging Pot   **(Sk)** Skillet

Drinks   ☐ Milk   ☐ Soda   ☐ Tea   ☐ Coffee   ☐ Drink Mix

Spices	**Condiments**	**Fruit**	**Nuts/Mix**	**Fixings**
☐ Salt	☐ Ketchup	☐ Apples	☐ Nuts/Seeds	☐ Lettuce
☐ Pepper	☐ Mustard	☐ Bananas	☐ Trail Mix	☐ Tomatoes
☐ Sugar	☐ Relish	☐ Oranges	☐ Power Bars	☐ Pickes
☐ Hot Sauce	☐ Salsa	☐ Grapefruit	☐ Fruit Bars	☐ Onions
☐ _____	☐ _____	☐ _____	☐ _____	☐ _____

POST-TRIP REVIEW

To make every camping trip better, it's important to capture and review what you liked and what you would change. Use this sheet to review and plan your next adventure.

Campground Name _____ Dates _____ To _____

Address Street _____ City _____ State _____

Type of Site/Park ☐ National ☐ State ☐ Private Campsite # _____

Types of Campsite ☐ Managed/RV ☐ Primitive ☐ Boondocking ☐ Wilderness

Types of Trip ☐ Basic Camping ☐ Glamping (Tent/Rental/RV)
☐ Bushcraft ☐ Primitive ☐ Combination

Sites/Excursions Along the Way

1 _____ 2 _____ 3 _____

Designated Tent / Pad Sites? ☐ Yes ☐ No Campsite # _____

Campground Amenities

☐ Drinking Water (close/far) ☐ Picnic   ☐ Firewood For Sale
☐ Fire Pits/Ring   ☐ Table – RV (120V 50A/30A)   ☐ Pet Friendly
☐ Tent Pads   ☐ Hookups   ☐ Nice Town
☐ BBQ Grill   ☐ Campground Store

What You Liked / What Went Well?

1 _____
2 _____

Other _____ Restrooms: Yes / No – Close / Far – Clean / Unclean – Shower / Electricity

What You Didn't Like / What Would You Change?

1 _____
2 _____

Animal Sightings _____

Biggest Surprise OR Need That The Campground Had (Or Didn't Have)? _____

Types of Activities Did You Do? (In Tent, Campsite, Campground, Local Areas, etc.)

_____

Things (activities / side trips) To Do Next Time?

_____

People You Met?

Name _____ From City/State _____ Phone/Email _____
Name _____ From City/State _____ Phone/Email _____
Name _____ From City/State _____ Phone/Email _____

Notes

_____

_____

_____

_____

_____

After arriving at your desired camping location, there are basically three phases to your adventure – set up, breaking camp, and post-trip storage. This information is from the book Camping, Glamping, Bushcraft 101 in the last section called "Let's Go Camping".

1   Setting Up Your Camp

The first thing to do when you arrive at your campsite is to pitch or build your shelter – tent, tarp, lean-to, or set up. Because of weather, darkness, animals, etc., you need a safe place to sleep.

1. Choose your tent/shelter location based on grade of land, rain flow, wind/storm, proximity to resources, and to avoid dangers such as large trees falling, mud slides, or flash floods.
2. Groundsheet – add/use a ground sheet (tarp) for protection (mud, bugs, thermal, punctures)
3. Quickly build your shelter before it gets dark, cold, or rains.
4. Organize kitchen, firewood, and other gear for protection against weather or varmints.

2   Breaking Camp – Time To Go

Hopefully you've just experienced another wonderful trip. Now it's time to pack, load, and go.

1. Prepare for leaving the night before – pack/load what you can, have last meal ready.
2. Disassemble tent or shelter in case the groundsheet or bottom needs to dry out.
3. Load gear same way as when leaving for trip – largest items first, emergency items easily reachable.
4. Keep emergency items (first aid kit, air compressor, rain suit, etc.) within easy and quick reach.
5. BUSHCRAFT breaking camp – move or change back anything built (shelter, fire ring, trapping devices, back to where "No human was here."
6. Triple-check fire and logs – cover with water or dirt, kick with boot/shovel, roll logs over, check again!
7. Walk campsite – form a line, follow a grid, pay your kids if they find trash or other things.
8. Check out with the park office or facilities if necessary.

3   Cleaning & Storing Gear

Your camping trip is not over until everything is packed and put away properly. Follow these 4 steps to make sure you protect your gear and are ready for your next great outdoor adventure.

Divide your gear/equipment into 4 different groups:

1. Items that can be stored right now – put them away.
2. Items that need to be cleaned or dried – moisture, mold, and rot will destroy camping gear.
3. Items that need to be fixed or repaired – order parts or replace.
4. Items that require power – recharge batteries, manage fuel (refill propane tanks – empty some fuels).

S.A.F.E. Survival™ Methodology

Outdoor activities such as camping, hiking, or water sports present inherent risks. Think about Safety First. Prepare a plan and carry the proper safety gear for emergencies before you embark. If a situation does occur, below is a 4-step process to assist you to stay safe or move to safety as fast as possible. Because every situation, environment, and resources are different, it is impossible to write out perfect answers and that is why following a consistent process is so important. Use these steps and framework as a method to minimize danger and improve outcomes by being smart.

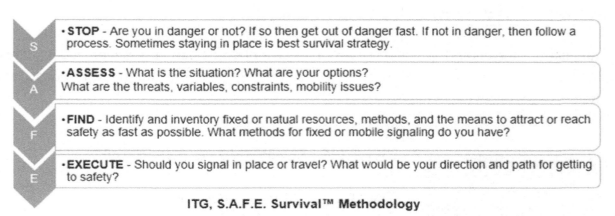

- **STOP** - Are you in danger or not? If so then get out of danger fast. If not in danger, then follow a process. Sometimes staying in place is best survival strategy.
- **ASSESS** - What is the situation? What are your options? What are the threats, variables, constraints, mobility issues?
- **FIND** - Identify and inventory fixed or natual resources, methods, and the means to attract or reach safety as fast as possible. What methods for fixed or mobile signaling do you have?
- **EXECUTE** - Should you signal in place or travel? What would be your direction and path for getting to safety?

ITG, S.A.F.E. Survival™ Methodology

Here is the methodology with examples from the hiking scenario in the book and becoming separated from your partner while on a trail in the woods.

STOP: Freeze! Unless you're under a situational threat (animal attack, flash flood, lightning, etc.), don't move. Before taking any physical actions, you must follow a process to become safe or get to safety. These 4 steps can be done in seconds to minutes. Remember, "HOW YOU THINK" is your most powerful tool to determine your survival and not let a bad situation become a catastrophe.

ASSESS: What are all your options and variables, like the remaining hours of light? How far is the reverse trailhead or trail marker? Will temperature or weather be a threat? What are constraints? What are additional risks? What happens if both of you become lost?

FIND: What resources do you have (on you and in nature) to lower risks and become safe? Can you signal your friend or others to help? Can you leave a message at your last point of separation with, "Where you went, when you will be back, what is the problem you need help with"?

EXECUTE: Follow your plan and strategy. Do you stay and use different types of signaling? If you go looking for them, leave information about where, and for how long. For example, a note that says, "I have done X, and I will return to this spot at the top of every hour." Or you hike out, leaving clear information on what you've done and if your friend comes back what they should do.

ADDITIONAL RESOURCES

Great camping, tent glamping, and wilderness living (Bushcraft) is much more than just location, equipment and gear. The most important camping tool you have is your level of knowledge – what you know and what you can apply.

To augment this robust planner, journal, and logbook here are three more important sources of knowledge and insights. This Planner, Journal, and Logbook is based off the book:

CAMPING, GLAMPING, & BUSHCRAFT 101
The Ultimate 3 in 1 Handbook
For Outdoor Camping Adventures
 Three formats:
✓ Hardcover
✓ Softcover Color
✓ Softcover B&W

YouTube Videos - www.youtube.com/@intentsglamping

Some of the most tricked out inflatable luxury tents and gear on the internet. Over 1 million views. Watch, subscribe, and share for knowledge and expertise.

Website - www.intentsglampingusa.com

Our website is a great resource for insights, information, blogs, and pictures of different camping set ups and resources.

Made in the USA
Coppell, TX
05 August 2024

35282644R10090